Paolo BOTTALLA

Pope Honorius before the Tribunal of Reason and History. A reply to "The Condemnation of Pope Honorius," by P. Le Page Renouf.

Paolo BOTTALLA

Pope Honorius before the Tribunal of Reason and History. A reply to "The Condemnation of Pope Honorius," by P. Le Page Renouf.

ISBN/EAN: 9783742816108

Manufactured in Europe, USA, Canada, Australia, Japa

Cover: Foto ©Andreas Hilbeck / pixelio.de

Manufactured and distributed by brebook publishing software (www.brebook.com)

Paolo BOTTALLA

Pope Honorius before the Tribunal of Reason and History. A reply to "The Condemnation of Pope Honorius," by P. Le Page Renouf.

PREFACE.

It had been the writer's intention, on issuing his recent work on the Supremacy of the Roman Pontiff, to follow up the argument by the publication of another volume on Papal Infallibility. But circumstances have led to an alteration in his plan, and have induced him to anticipate a little, and at once publish an Essay on the supposed fall and heresy of Pope Honorius. This change is rendered advisable by the pamphlet of Mr. P. Le Page Renouf, which appeared in May last, entitled *The Condemnation of Pope Honorius.* Mr. Renouf has not been satisfied with following in the steps of Dr. Döllinger in that writer's unfortunate crusade against Papal Infallibility; he must aim yet higher. He believes that "an influential party in the Church is looking forward with impatience to the day in which their favourite dogma (Papal Infallibility) shall be defined as an article of faith, introduced into our Catechism, and made obligatory under pain of anathem upon all the children of the Church."¹ He seems to suppose himself, on this account, to have received from on high the mission of giving the alarm to all the theologians of the Catholic world that Ultramontanism is preparing to win a new victory over the opposite party. He, a layman, without any solid foundation of theological study, comes forward to caution Catholic theologians against the artifices prepared and the snares laid for them; he informs them that they are about to be led to reject "the old maxim of Vincent of Lerins, 'quod semper, quod ubique, quod ab omnibus,' as a test of Catholic doctrine;" that they will have to "abjure the Creed of Pope Pius, according to which they have sworn that they will never interpret Scripture otherwise than according to the unanimous consent of the Fathers."² He is therefore good enough to instruct them that there is not a single Father who favours the Ultramontane theory of Papal Infallibility; not a Council which has believed it;³ that "the existence of such privilege was in fact never heard of till after the separation of the East from the West;"⁴ that the doctrine of Papal Infallibility was not consistently developed before the sixteenth

---

¹ The Condemnation of Pope Honorius, p. 27; London, 1868.
² Ib. p. 28.   ³ Ib. pp. 28-30.   ⁴ Ib. p. 30.

century;⁵ but rather "elaborated in that age;"⁶ that Ultramontanism is of recent date, for the greater proportion of the medieval theologians rejected an opinion, afterwards adopted by writers whose "combined weight cannot even tend to make an article of faith."⁷ The bold assertions heaped up by Mr. Renouf *in tribus pagellis* is not so amazing as the tone of contempt and the unbecoming and even outrageous language which he adopts towards the most learned theologians, and the whole body of Catholic writers who have attempted to defend Papal Infallibility, whether in general, or in the particular case of Pope Honorius. "They represent," Mr. Renouf tells us, "a pseudo-scientific method of reasoning in theology;"⁸ "they strangely misunderstand the spirit of St. Thomas, whom they ignorantly admire;"⁹ "they betray an utter ignorance of the real nature of the controversy;"¹⁰ "they altogether misrepresent the matter."¹¹ He condemns in the strongest terms their "ignorant assertions, which have been," as he says, "common of late;"¹² he attributes to them "bad arguments," "monstrous forms of hypothesis," "miserable evasions, which cannot have been sincerely believed in by their authors."¹³ He goes still fur-

⁵ The Condemnation of Pope Honorius, p. 31. ⁶ Ib. p. 7.
⁷ Ib. pp. 37, 38. ⁸ l. c. ⁹ l. c. ¹⁰ Ib. p. 14.
¹¹ Ib. p. 23. ¹² Ib. p. 1 note. ¹³ Ib. pp. 7, 10, 24.

ther. Without a particle of that reserve which common courtesy, if no other feeling, ought to have suggested, he accuses them of falsehood, of stupid bigotry, of dishonesty. "It is a simple untruth," he asserts, "to say that Honorius was condemned for neglect."[14] Yet he ought to know that, at the present day, this is the opinion most commonly held among Catholics. "It is a sheer dishonesty," he adds in the next page, "to shut one's eyes to the strongest words of the Council."[15] "It is stupid bigotry to assert," he says in another place, "that Honorius was in good faith."[16] In such terms does this civil-spoken writer charge the bulk of modern theologians with bigotry and dishonesty. He speaks yet more plainly of F. Perrone, the well-known Professor of Theology at the Roman College; he cites a passage from the *Prælectiones Theologicæ*, naming the author, and then remarks upon it, "under this contemptible quibbling we have the assertion of an untruth."[17] To speak thus contemptuously of the great mass of Catholic theologians is not only unbecoming a Catholic writer, but also, we make bold to say, it ill suits the character of an English gentleman; and persons of all religions should join

[14] The Condemnation of Pope Honorius, p. 11.
[15] Ib. p. 12.   [16] Ib. p. 18.   [17] Ib. p. 24 note.

Preface. ix

in reprobating the use of such language. Mr. Renouf has no words of praise or commendation for any of the Catholic writers who belong to what he calls the Ultramontane school; but he exalts to the skies all those who were the promoters of Gallicanism.

He gives the epithet of *great* to the well-known *Defensio Declarationis Cleri Gallicani*, by which book he thinks "the Ultramontane theory may be said to have been thoroughly exploded."[18] He calls *excellent* the book of Cardinal de la Luzerne on the declaration of the French clergy in 1682, in attempted refutation of Cardinal Orsi's work on Papal Authority and Infallibility.[19] "All the learned priests he met in France," he asserts, "or indeed heard of, were determined Gallicans, and they were men of eminent piety."[20] On the contrary, the founder of the *Univers*, who, as he believes, "brought a large portion of the French clergy to share his own view" (of Ultramontanism), is described by him as "a fiery, ignorant, and unscrupulous convert from unbelief or indifference."[21] He seems to lament that "the most ardent apostles of Ultramontane theories have been laymen rather than priests, converts rather than men who have always been Catholics."[22] We are

[18] The Condemnation of Pope Honorius, p. 38.
[19] Ib. note. [20] Ib. p. 39. [21] L c. [22] l. c.

able to give him some comfort by the assurance that neither is the success of Ultramontanism in Germany wholly due to the influence of Görres and Windischmann, nor "was the impulse to it first given in England by the *Tablet*, under the editorship of two ardent converts, who were for a long time a terror to the ecclesiastical authorities."[28] We are fully convinced that in Germany, as well as in England, the Catholic Clergy would indignantly reject so groundless an assertion. But how is it that, whilst Mr. Renouf bitterly deplores the influence of laymen in these affairs, he, a layman, appears to aim at the leadership of the English Catholic Clergy in a career of upholding Gallican theories? We do not take upon ourselves to judge the private intentions of the author: we judge his pamphlet, which, by its dogmatic tone, certainly appears to manifest some such hopes. Even if this were not Mr. Renouf's intention, how is it that he, a Catholic, comes forward to arouse the rebellious spirits of this country against the infallible authority of the Vicar of Christ? Does he think that the English Catholic Clergy want *scientific* advice, or that they are willing to receive it at his hands? We have formed far too high an estimate of their solidity in holding Catholic principles to be

[28] The Condemnation of Pope Honorius, p. 40.

able to harbour such an idea of them. We are sure that the Catholic Clergy of England have one opinion concerning Mr. Renouf's conduct,—namely, that he need not trouble himself with Catholic controversies; that he may safely leave to them the care of theological matters; and that he may hope for better success in his labours if he confine himself to Egyptian philology.

We should have taken no notice of the immoderate and insulting language of Mr. Renouf, had he not mixed it up with a heap of undigested difficulties against Papal Infallibility. By such an accumulation of charges, without any order or explanation whatever, simple people may be easily led into error. Therefore it is necessary to clear up, analyse, and examine as to their bearing and purport, such difficulties and charges. But as this cannot be done within the limits of a pamphlet, and since we hope shortly to publish the second part of our work—*The Pope and the Church*—on Papal Infallibility, we will refer to it for the explanation of those difficulties which Mr. Renouf has scraped together from some half-forgotten books, and then dressed up with the purpose of proving that Papal Infallibility is untenable. At present we limit ourselves to pleading the cause of Pope Honorius, against whom Mr. Renouf's pamphlet is principally aimed. We are glad to assume the position of humble followers of such men as Mamachius, Baronius, Pagi, Petavius, Garnier, Thomassini, Bellarmine, Natalis Alexander, Orsi, Ballerini, and other theologians of the greatest reputation for learning, who, in defending the cause of Pope Honorius, have defended Papal Infallibility; and we are proud to take to ourselves a part of those outrageous invectives which Mr. Renouf does not blush to cast upon some of the most eminent writers which the Catholic Church has produced.

CONTENTS.

I.

Origin and Nature of Monothelism, pp. 1-16.

Monophytism: its persistency, growth, and power for three centuries; it enervated the Empire and threatened it with ruin—Heraclius endeavours to save the State from destruction; he is gained over by Sergius to favour Monothelism with the political view of uniting the religious factions—Three patriarchates in the hands of the Monothelites—Sophronius resists in Alexandria and in Jerusalem—Sergius has recourse to Pope Honorius against Sophronius—The heretics who first denied two operations and wills in Christ—The new Monothelites a section of the Monophysites, although giving an outward assent to the formula of Chalcedon—Similarity of the dogma of the Monothelites with that of Severus—Both heresies the product of Apollinarism—Artifices of the Monothelites to conceal and to propagate their dogma—Summary.

II.

The two Letters written by Honorius to Sergius: their true character, pp. 16-44.

Double aspect of the controversy concerning Honorius' two letters to Sergius—Characters of a Papal document *ex cathedrâ* in a matter of faith—Honorius' two letters devoid of these distinctive marks—Sergius did not apply to the Pope for a final decision in the matter; he is hindered from doing so by motives of prudence—Summary of Sergius' letter to Honorius: he insists only on an œconomical abstinence from the use of the words, "one or two operations in Christ"—Honorius consents to his proposal, but defines nothing; his letters devoid of synodical character; not intended for the instruction of all the Church: therefore long remained unknown in the archives of Constantinople—Second embassy sent by Sophronius to Pope Honorius; that Pope dead when it reached Rome—Remarks on the embassy—Mr. Renouf's mistake concerning doctrinal definitions.

III.

Orthodox Doctrines contained in the two Letters of Pope Honorius to Sergius, pp. 45-80.

De Marca's judgment on the orthodoxy of Pope Honorius—The calumniators of that Pope—Capital dogma of Monothelism, the assertion of one operation in Christ—The contrary doctrine was clearly proposed by St. Leo in his dogmatical letter—The letters of Pope Honorius set forth the identical doctrine of St. Leo—In Sergius' letter to Honorius the Monothalite dogma is plainly advocated—Further explanation of the Catholic doctrine on the Incarnation contained in Honorius' letters—He excluded from Christ only the "will of the flesh"—True explanation which he gives of the text, "Non quod ego volo," &c.—New mistake of Mr. Renouf in the matter—Evidences in favour of the foregoing explanation of Honorius' letters—Authority and honesty of the witnesses referred to defended against the false imputations of Dr. Döllinger and Mr. Renouf—No similarity whatever between the letters of Honorius and the *Ecthesis* and *Typus*—Their contradictory nature—Contemporary witnesses of Honorius' orthodoxy—The Council of Lateran under Martin I.—It furnishes a proof of the orthodoxy of Honorius.

IV.

The Sixth Synod and the Condemnation of Pope Honorius, pp. 80-136.

Great evils caused in the Eastern Church by Monothelism—The Greek Emperors persecute the Catholics and support the schism—Constantine Pogonatus begs from the Pope a General Council for the peace of the Church—It meets at Constantinople—The Emperor held in it the first place of honour, not of right—The Papal Legates are instructed to set before the Synod the certain and unchangeable doctrine of the Roman See—Pope Agatho's letters to the Emperor and to the Council clearly state the doctrine of Papal Infallibility in its principles and its practice—The Fathers of the Sixth Council are compelled to submit to the Papal decisions, under threat of reprobation—They submit to all the Papal conclusions in the completest manner—They profess the same full submission before and after Honorius' condemnation—consequently they could not have condemned this Pope for error *ex cathedrâ*—Inquiry into the real offence for which Honorius was condemned—Passages of the Synod in which he is condemned apart from the Monothelite heretics, and other passages in which he is condemned in common with the rest—Examination of the decree of his condemnation—The cause of his condemnation is advisedly distinguished by that document from that of the Monothelites—In it, as well as in the others, it is placed in his having followed Sergius in all his designs—True meaning of these words—Real crime of Honorius—The difficulty brought by Mr. Renouf is answered—Examination of the passages in which he is condemned in common with the others—In what sense Honorius partook of the same fault *in solidum* with the others, although guilty of no heresy whatever—Mr. Renouf's injudicious appeal to Pyrrhus' and Macarius' testimony against Honorius—Additional remarks on the address of the Sixth Synod to Pope Agatho concerning Honorius' condemnation—Conduct of the Council in condemning that Pope—The Roman See never authorised the Synod to condemn Honorius as a heretic—Pope Leo II. sanctioned only the definition of faith of the Council, and manifestly upheld Papal Infallibility—In his letter of confirmation of the Council the fault of Honorius is attributed to grievous neglect in the discharge of his duty—Pope Leo inculcated the same in his letters to the Bishops of Spain and to King Ervigius—Misrepresentation of a passage of the letter by Mr. Renouf—The *Liber Diurnus* tells in favour of Honorius' orthodoxy—Opinions of Garnier and De Marca in the matter—From the second profession of faith a new confirmation is given of his orthodoxy—Examination of the fourth lesson of the old Roman Breviary for the Feast of St. Leo II.—In older Latin Breviaries no name is mentioned of those who were condemned by the Sixth Synod—The lessons for that feast are copied word for word from St. Leo's Life, written by Anastasius—This writer was one of the most zealous defenders of Honorius' orthodoxy, and could not say of him that he had denied the two wills and operations in Christ—Anastasius made a summary of the condemnation of the Sixth Synod from St.

Leo's letter to Constantine; but he suppressed the grounds of the several condemnations mentioned in it—The words, "qui unam voluntatem et operationem in D. N. J. C. dixerunt," &c. do not concern Honorius or any of those named, but only the last class of heretics, as in Leo's letter and in the second profession of faith in the *Liber Diurnus*—Not correct to say that Honorius' name was expunged in the reformed Roman Breviary, and the others retained; nor would it have been unjust to expunge it—Purport of the anathemas inflicted on Honorius by the Seventh and Eighth Councils—They did not condemn that Pope for any erroneous teaching *ex cathedrâ*, nor for any heresy of any kind—The Seventh Synod has nothing in its profession of faith and in its Synodical Letter to the Emperor which tells against Honorius' orthodoxy—The Eighth Council intended only to confirm the sentence pronounced in the Sixth Synod—True meaning of the anathema inflicted on Honorius—His name was never erased from the diptychs.

Conclusion, pp. 135-149.

Double object of this apology for Honorius—How his name deserves veneration and gratitude in England—Method followed in the argument—Character of Mr. Renouf's pamphlet—The term of "Ultramontane" given by him to the immense majority of Catholics—He seems to maintain that the Pope is subject to the civil ruler—If he means in civil matters, no one teaches a different doctrine; if he means in ecclesiastical matters (and this appears to be his opinion), he is wrong—Refutation of the opinion.

POPE HONORIUS BEFORE THE TRIBUNAL OF REASON AND HISTORY.

I.

Origin and Nature of Monothelism.

THE great controversy concerning the Incarnation, which for three centuries raged in the Oriental Church with a violence bordering upon madness, relates to the subject of the two natures in Christ. No heresy caused more calamitous disasters to the Church and the Empire during the first seven centuries than the one called Monophysite. It struck its roots so deeply and strongly in the East, that neither the authoritative Dogmatic Letter of the great Pope Leo, nor the Œcumenical Council of Chalcedon, aided even by the zeal of the virtuous Emperor Marcian, could succeed in extirpating it. Indeed, after the general council of Chalcedon, it spread with a new growth, and developed itself with a fresh vigour. It invaded the patriarchate of Jerusalem; it overflowed into those of Alexandria and Antioch, and enthroned its adherents in the patriarchal sees; it was supported by the Patriarch of Constantinople himself,—nay even by the successors of Marcian on the imperial throne. The famous ἑνωτικόν of the Emperor Zeno was evidently in favour of the heresy, though it originated new divisions and schisms among the sectarians. The persecutions of the Emperor Anastasius against the defenders of the faith of Chalcedon, and the deplorable Acacian schism, helped to consolidate its existence and widen its influence. Notwithstanding the exertions of the Emperors Justin II. and Justinian I., and of the Bishops assembled in the fifth general council in Constantinople, no means were discovered of reconciling the Monophysite heretics with the doctrine of the Synod of Chalcedon. The defenders of one nature in Christ, although broken up into manifold minor parties,—such as Severians, Julianists, Agnoëtes, Theodosians, Jacobites, Copts,—were spread in large numbers over Syria, Mesopotamia, Asia Minor, Cyprus, Palestine, as well as Armenia and Egypt; and as these factions were in the ascendant, they appointed their own patriarchs to the sees of Alexandria, of Antioch, and of Firjin in Armenia. The supreme influence which the Monophysites had gained, and which extended into the provinces of the Eastern Empire, and the violent hatred they entertained against the Catholics, had become a continued danger, and a standing menace to the Court of Constantinople. The Empire was at that time exposed to the savage incursions of the Persians on one side, and of the Arabs on the other. During the sixth century the Arabs had forced its frontier, and, bursting into Egypt, had

Origin and Nature of Monothelism. 3

devastated the country far and wide. At the same time the Persian armies had advanced westward; and in the first part of the seventh century, after having ravaged Syria, Palestine, and Africa as far as Carthage, had showed themselves on the shores of the Bosphorus within sight of the walls of Constantinople (621). So that if the Monophysites of Syria, Palestine, and Asia Minor had preferred the strong yoke of these barbarians to the effeminate rule of the Greek Empire, far advanced in its decadence, the Byzantine power would soon have fallen into ruin. It was well known that during the invasion of Egypt by the Arabs the Monophysite influence had been exercised in favour of the Saracens, who in turn had assisted their partisans to obtain possession of the Alexandrine patriarchate. But the mere existence of these sectarians was a perpetual source of domestic trouble. Their frequent risings were not suppressed without much bloodshed, and the strength of the Empire was thus enervated and rendered more and more unable to cope with its enemies from without.

Such was the state of things at the accession of Heraclius. The ascendency of the Monophysites on the one side, and the alarming invasions of the Persian armies on the other, made him anxious to effect a reconciliation between the Catholics and the heretics, that so he might be able to make head against the foreign enemy, and preserve the Empire from utter ruin. But whilst Heraclius, led by political reasons, sought for union in his states, some Bishops, who had long before imbibed the poison of the Monophysite heresy, conceived the design of reproducing its fundamental dogma under a different form, and of forcing it as a law upon the Church, under the plausible show of a means well adapted to reconcile the Monophysites with the Catholics. The formula under which the old Monophysite error was to be disguised asserted the unity of operations in Christ (μια ἐστιν ἡ ἐνέργεια τοῦ Χριστοῦ). Sergius, Patriarch of Constantinople, seems to have been the first to conceive this formula as a means of securing the desired reconciliation and union; and therefore the sixth general council said that he was the first to propagate the new error by his writings.[1] It is certain that the Emperor Heraclius was gained over to the new formula, and saw in it a means well calculated to establish concord between Monophysites and Catholics, and to give the Empire internal peace, and with it strength and power. From that time the new heresy gained consistency and support, Sergius and Heraclius being its most zealous apostles. In a short time all the leaders of the Monophysite sects were won over to the formula, and upon this basis they admitted the confession of the two natures in Christ. Thus Theodorus, Bishop of Pharan in Arabia, Paul and Athanasius, — the former being head of the Armenian Monophysites, the

---

[1] Conc. Constantinop. iii. Œcum. vi. act. xiii. Labbe, t. vii. pp. 977, 980. But the Libellus of Stephen of Dora, read in the Council of Lateran I., ascribed the origin of that heresy to Theodorus of Pharan. Conc. Lat. Secr. ii. (Labbe, t. vii. p. 106.)

latter chiefs of those of Syria,—were persuaded to embrace the new formula. Even Cyrus, Bishop of Phasis, was induced by the artfulness of Sergius to subscribe to it, and as a price of his apostasy was appointed Patriarch of Alexandria by Heraclius, as Athanasius had been rewarded with the patriarchal see of Antioch. In this manner the new heresy was enthroned, in the course of a few years, in the three patriarchates of Constantinople, Alexandria, and Antioch, and shielded with the imperial protection. Athanasius of Antioch, having attained the object of his ambition, laboured for the reconciliation of the Jacobites. Cyrus of Alexandria brought the Theodosians of Egypt to terms of concord by means of a formal treaty, consisting of nine articles, the seventh of which had reference to the new doctrine of one operation in Christ;[2] whilst Sergius, who was the centre and the life of all the movement, encouraged and supported his adherents in their deceitful task, and raised up new enemies against the confession of Chalcedon. He sought to enforce by imperial law a reconciliation which could not possibly be lasting so long as it rested merely on the basis of error and heresy. But the courageous resistance of Sophronius, a monk of Alexandria, deranged for a while the designs of this arch-heretic. Sophronius had in vain implored the Patriarch of Alexandria not to give publicity to the articles signed by the Theodosians. To the learned monk Sergius replied, that

[†] See them in the Sixth Œcum. Conc. act. xiii. (Labbe, t. vii. p. 987.)

the peace of the Church and of the Empire imperiously demanded this condescension to be shown to the Monophysites. Nevertheless, he was well aware that a policy of silence afforded the only hope of bringing to a successful issue his deceitful and heretical labour of reconciliation. He wrote to this effect to Cyrus of Alexandria, and gave the same advice to the Emperor Heraclius.

But the zealous Sophronius did not allow himself to be entangled in the snares of the patriarch. From his convent in Palestine he wrote strongly against the new heresy, and when raised to the patriarchal chair of Jerusalem, assembled all the Bishops under his jurisdiction, and pronounced anathema against the new error of one operation and will in Christ.[a] The election of Sophronius to the patriarchal see of Jerusalem, and much more his first synod against Monothelism, could not fail to awaken grave misgivings in the mind of the Patriarch of Constantinople, for he feared that the influence of his own authority, even with the support of the two Patriarchs of Alexandria and Antioch, would prove insufficient to counteract the zeal and vigour of his saintly opponent. Therefore, in order to prop up the falling edifice of Monothelism some more powerful influence was needed, and this could be found nowhere but in Rome, in the countenance of the supreme Head of the Church and Father of all Fathers. Sergius was so strongly persuaded of this, that even before the Synod of Jerusalem he had addressed a most insidious

[a] See Libell. Synod. (Labbo, t. vi. p. 1441.)

Origin and Nature of Monothelism.

letter to Pope Honorius, whose support he sought in favour of his policy of silence, hoping thus to counteract the opposition of Sophronius. But before examining his letter and the answer given to it by Pope Honorius, it will be well to have a clear understanding of the exact question raised by the Monothelites.

The error of one operation and one will in Christ is, in its substance, of ancient date in the Church. Long before the Monothelites, Beron, and after him the Arians, had denied two operations and two wills in Christ: the former taught that our Lord's human nature was swallowed up by the divine; the latter maintained that the Word supplied the functions of the soul in His humanity.[4] Apollinaris had also inculcated the same doctrine, in order to show that the flesh of Christ was consubstantial with His divinity, capable consequently of suffering.[5] On the other hand, as early as the third century, the Catholic doctrine of the two operations and wills in Christ had been clearly understood and accurately propounded by the early Fathers of the Church, among whom St. Hippolytus, in his fragments against Beron, had spoken of it with great precision.[6] He and all the others who had treated the matter had laid down the important maxim, that identity of operation would imply identity of na-

[4] See Petavius, Theol. Dogm. t. iv. De Incarnat. l. viii. c. iii. n. 1, 2, p. 339. Venetiis, 1757.
[5] See Petavius, l. c. n. 3, p. 339 seq.
[6] Fragmenta S. Hippolyti M. Fragm. v. (Galland. t. ii. p. 468.)

ture.⁷ And unquestionably all the early heretics who had held the doctrine of one operation and one will in Christ had either implicitly or explicitly denied the two natures. This was the case in the instances above given of Beron, the Arians, and the Apollinarists; for human nature deprived of all its powers, and animated and moved as a material and inactive instrument by the Logos, cannot be truly termed a human nature, much less a distinct and perfect human nature; that kind of union would result either in the total destruction of one nature, or in a coalition of both into something compounded of the two. Therefore the Monophysites, and especially Severus with his partisans, deprived Christ of a double natural will and operation, in order that they might deprive Him of His human nature. Severus did not deny the essence and the reality of manhood in Christ, but held the doctrine of a substantial change in its qualities from the in-flow of the Word of God into the sacred humanity.⁸ Consequently he anathematised the dogmatic letter of St. Leo and the confession of Chalcedon, because these taught two natures and two operations in Christ after the hypostatical union of His Godhead with His humanity.⁹ Theodosius of Alexandria, the leader of the Theodosians, laid down the same doctrine in his address to

⁷ See Petavius, op. cit. 1. viii. c. i. n. 5 seq. p. 336 seq. cc. viii. ix. pp. 350-357.
⁸ S. Maximus, Opuscula ad Marianum, p. 39 seq. 50 seq. Op. t. ii. ed. Migne.
⁹ Conc. (Œcum. vi. act. iv. Epist. Agathonis Papæ. (Labbe, t. vii. p. 691.)

the Empress Theodora, with whom he was in favour;[10] and as a general statement we may say that Monophysites of every faction professed the same dogma. The heretic Anthimus also deduced the unity of operation and will in Christ from the unity of His incarnate nature.[11] Thus we have sufficient proof that the Monothelites were really a section only of the Monophysites. Theodore of Pharan and Athanasius were certainly both Monophysites; Sergius himself was born in Syria, of Jacobite parents; and when these agreed upon upholding the dogma of one operation in Christ, they must have grounded their teaching on the unity of His nature as well as of His person. For, as Theophanes remarks, "they knew well that where one operation is admitted, there must one nature be acknowledged."[12] Consequently Cyrus of Phasis also must have been well acquainted with that doctrine at the time when he yielded to the suggestions of Sergius and became a fiery promoter of the Monothelite tenets for the sake of the proffered patriarchal see. Moreover, after the solemn reconciliation of the Theodosians and Jacobites with the Catholics, the former publicly boasted, as Theophanes testifies, "that the Council of Chalcedon had entered their communion, not themselves that of Chalcedon;" and that the unity

[10] Ib. p. 694, ot Conc. Lat. act. v. (Labbe, t. vi. p. 323-328.)
[11] Ib. act. xi. (Labbe, t. vii. p. 937.)
[12] Theophanes Chronographia ad an. 621, p. 506-7. ed. Bonn. ἰγίνωσκιν γὰρ ὅτι ἱνὰ μία ἐνέργεια εἴρηται, ἐκεῖ καὶ μία φύσις γνωρίζεται.

10   *Origin and Nature of Monothelism.*

of operation being once admitted in Christ, they would be able to hold and teach the oneness of His nature.[13] Therefore in the Council of Lateran, as well as in the sixth general synod, it was truly said that the Monothelites had renewed, by their errors, the dogmas of Apollinaris and Severus.[14] Nevertheless the Monothelites professed externally to admit the faith of Chalcedon, and solemnly acknowledged two natures in Christ. Thus Cyrus of Alexandria made this profession in all the above-quoted articles of the concord concluded with the Theodosians, except the seventh, on the wills and operations in Christ. Macarius of Antioch made the same in his confession of faith, read in the Sixth Council.[15] So did all the leaders of that sect, whose professions of faith exist both in the Council of Lateran and the third of Constantinople. But this need not surprise us : Eutyches himself, in the synod held at Constantinople under Flavian, asserted that Christ was perfect God and perfect Man ;[16] and yet it is well known that he was condemned in the Council of Chalcedon because he admitted in Christ a com-

---

[13] κατεκαυχῶντο γὰρ οἱ Ἰακωβῖται καὶ οἱ Θεοδοσιανοὶ φάσκοντες ὅτι οὐχ ἡμεῖς τῇ Χαλκηδόνι, ἀλλ' ἡ Χαλκηδὼν μᾶλλον ἡμῖν ἐκοινώνησεν, διὰ τῆς μιᾶς ἐνεργείας μίαν ὁμολογήσασα φύσιν Χριστοῦ. Theoph. op. cit. 1. c. p. 507.

[14] Libellus Stephani Dorensis, in Conc. Lat. sub Martino I. Secr. ii. (Labbe, t. vii. p. 105.) Secr. iv. (l. c. p. 270.) Conc. vi. Const. act. iv. Ep. Agathonis Papæ. (Labbe, l. c. p. 692.)

[15] Conc. Œcum. vi. act. viii. (Labbe, t. vii. p. 769.)

[16] Conc. Constantinop. sub Flaviano Patriarcha, act. iii. In Actis Conc. Chalced. act. i. (Labbe, t. iv. p. 976.) καὶ ταῦτα λέγων τέλειον Θεὸν εἶναι καὶ τέλειον ἄνθρωπον.

pound nature, such as would undoubtedly destroy both the Godhead and the Manhood. When a formula of Christian faith has been preserved through centuries, from generation to generation, and has become in a manner a part of the mind of the Church, the denial of it would argue consummate impudence, and must meet with opposition if not contempt. Now such a formula was that of "perfect God" and "perfect Man" in Christ. After the Council of Chalcedon, the Monophysites repudiated the system of physical composition of two natures in Christ, as taught by Eutyches. They understood perfectly that to give any plausibility to their error they must retain the time-honoured form of words; and when the authors of the Monothelite system offered the Monophysites admission to Catholic communion, on the easy condition of admitting the ancient formula of perfect God and perfect Man in Christ, which had been long before sanctioned at Chalcedon, they could not refuse to accept terms which would leave them still at liberty to carry on their work of mischief.

The new error, in real truth, of the Monothelites differed from that of the Severians in this only—that what the elder sect derived as a corollary from a principle, was in the new system the fundamental principle itself. From the earliest period of their existence, they maintained in plain terms that there is only one operation, as there is only one person, in Jesus Christ. All the documents referred to, both in the Council of Lateran and in the Sixth Œcumenical

12 *Origin and Nature of Monothelism.*

Synod, point to this teaching:[17] all the leaders of the heresy, from the very first, spoke distinctly of one operation in Christ, μία ἐνέργεια, though some maintained likewise the unity of His will.[18] The word ἐνέργεια, although it is not unfrequently used by the Greeks in the sense of ἐνέργημα (an external act), still is more commonly used to express the operating principle, δύναμις, substantial, essential to the nature itself which it enables to act. So that, as we have said, it was a very common maxim among the ancient Fathers, that no nature can exist without its natural principle of operation, ἐνέργεια. Now the Monothelites absolutely denied this principle of operation in the human nature of Christ; and although they acknowledged that it possessed soul and body, with the faculties of each, still they plainly asserted that these were unable to perform any operation whatever by themselves; since all the operations both of the human and of the divine nature were to be ascribed to the power of the Divine Word, who was personally united with the humanity. They maintained, therefore, without disguise, that the human nature in Christ was only an instrument of His Divinity;[19]

[17] Excerpta ex Scriptis Theodori Pharanitæ. In Secr. iii. Conc. Lat. (Labbe, t. vii. pp. 170-71) et in act. xiii. Conc. Gen. vi. (Labbe, l. c. p. 991 seq.) Capitulum vii. Cyri Alex. In Secr. iii. Conc. Lat. (l. c. p. 181), in act. xiii. Conc. Gen. vi. (l. c. p. 988-89. Epist. Sergii ad Cyrum Patr., in Secr. iii. Conc. Lat. (l. c. p. 184), in Conc. Gen. vi. act. xii. (l. c. pp. 948-49). Epist. Cyri ad Sergium. In Conc. Gen. vi. act. xiii. (l. c. p. 983), &c.
[18] Among them is Theodorus of Pharan. See Excerpta in Conc. Lat. l. c. p. 169.
[19] μίαν γινώσκειν ἐνέργειαν, ταύτης δὲ τεχνίτην καὶ δημιουργὸν τὸν

Origin and Nature of Monothelism. 13

consequently they acknowledged no other understanding and will in Christ than that of the Logos, from whom the operation and power of the soul flowed or proceeded. The humanity of Christ without the Logos was compared by them to a senseless body without a soul.[20] Nay, they went so far as to teach that the body of Christ was devoid of every principle of movement and action. Of course they admitted that our Lord suffered in His flesh, and they repudiated the error of Apollinaris, that the Divine nature was capable of suffering; but at the same time they professed that although the physical impression was received by the flesh, nevertheless its vital power of operation, ἐνέργεια, upon which sensation depends, was entirely supplied by the Divine substance of the Logos.[21] This monstrous doctrine was copied literally by Sergius and Theodorus from Apollinaris, as can be seen by the extracts from his writings read both in the Council of Lateran and in the third of Constantinople.[22] They were too cun-

---

Θεὸν, ὄργανον δὲ τὴν ἀνθρωπότητα. Theodorus of Pharan. In Conc. Gen. vi. act. xiii. (Labbe, t. c. p. 993.) See also the other extracts in that place.

[20] Sergius Epist. ad Honorium Papam. In act. iii. Conc. (Labbe, t. vii. p. 957.)

[21] Theodorus Pharan. Excerpta. In act. xiii. Conc. vi. (Labbe, t. vii. p. 992). Sergius, l. c. Epist. Cyri ad Sergium. In act. xiii. Conc. vi. (Labbe, l. c. p. 984). Macarius, Professio fidei lecta in act. viii. Conc. vi. (Labbe, l. c. p. 776), &c.

[22] Θεὸς ἀναλαβὼν ὄργανον καὶ Θεός ἐστι καθ᾿ ἐνέργειᾳ, καὶ ἄνθρωπος κατὰ τὸ ὄργανον. μόνον δὲ Θεὸς οὐ μεταβέβληται ὄργανον καὶ τὸ κινοῦν μίαν πέφυκεν ἀποστέλλειν τὴν ἐνέργειαν. In Conc. Gen. vi. act. x. (Labbe, l. c. p. 872.)

ning, however, not to conceal the true source of their heresy, and appealed to the doctrine of the Fathers of the Church, especially to the writings which bear the name of St. Denis the Areopagite. But this holy doctor never taught that in Christ there was only one will, much less one operation. He taught that there were in Christ theandric operations—an expression which implies the two natures as separate principles of action, though in fact always acting together. But he never thought of asserting one theandric operation in Christ, so as to exclude all operating power from His humanity, and to reduce it to the state of an inoperative instrument of the Divinity. Sergius endeavoured to pervert a Catholic doctrine, and to shelter himself under the authority of St. Leo, hoping thus to throw dust into the eyes of the Catholics, and to insinuate his error as orthodox doctrine. It is true, as he maintained, that the Godhead is the leading and ruling principle of the sacred humanity; but this does not mean that because the governing principle ever comes from the Person of the eternal Logos, therefore operation (ἐνέργεια) must flow from the same upon an inactive and insensible humanity. It is true, again, that human nature in Christ loses its independence, so far as to require the permission of the Divine Person in order to elicit its actions; but notwithstanding this, it keeps its natural freedom, preserves in its integrity the substantial power of operating, and acts from and through that power. The theandric operations, if referred to the Person of Christ, terminate in the unity of that Person; but considered in themselves are never so blended and united as to form a principle of action which is single in its essence. The same must be said of the two wills of Christ. The Monothelites, therefore, whilst they denied the natural will of the humanity of Christ (τὸ θέλημα φυσικὸν), advocated one practical and personal will (τὸ θέλημα γνωμικὸν, ὑποστατικὸν), and they hoped thus to be successful in deceiving the multitude, by conveying the impression that they merely wished to avoid the error of two contrary and conflicting wills in Christ, whilst in reality they absolutely denied the existence of the will in His human nature. On this account they were less reserved when maintaining one personal will in Christ than when defending one operation in Him. For it was well known that the word operation (ἐνέργεια) is commonly taken for what is substantial in every nature; and that consequently by denying the two operations in Christ, they would be convicted of denying along with these the reality of the two natures: since there is no nature or substance, if it be deprived of all physical operation (ἀνενέργητος).[23] Moreover, they endeavoured to justify their error by the argument, that the existence of two wills in the one indivisible Person of Christ implied a state of struggle and conflict in Him.[24]

[23] See Petavius, Theol. Dogm. t. iv. De Incarnat. l. i. c. xxi. § viii. p. 48.
[24] This argument is common to all the leaders of the heresy. See Epist. Sergii ad Honorium Papam, in act. xiii. Conc. Gen. vi. l. c. Macarii Professio fidei. In act. viii. Conc. Gen. vi. (Labbe, t. vii. p. 775.)

To sum up, then; we may reduce the errors of the Monothelites to the three following heads: 1st, they acknowledged in Christ one sole divine operation pervading the sacred humanity which was merely its instrument. 2dly, as a consequence, they did not acknowledge in Christ more than one sole divine will. 3dly, implicitly, and as a further consequence, they admitted the capital error of the Monophysites, especially that particular form of it which characterised the followers of Severus.

II.

The two Letters written by Honorius to Sergius; their true character.

The controversy upon which we have entered may be considered as presenting a double aspect; one concerns directly the infallibility of the Pope, the other regards principally the integrity of the faith of Honorius. In other words, it may be asked whether Honorius in his two famous letters taught Monothelism as Pope and *ex cathedrâ*, and whether he personally and as a "doctor privatus" fell into that heresy at all. A further inquiry may be made, whether the Sixth Council and the Popes who confirmed it condemned Honorius as having taught heresy in the full exercise of his papal authority, or for some other grievous fault committed in the discharge of his apostolical ministry. The opponents of papal infallibility seek to uphold their cause by the help of the supposed fall of Honorius; and for this purpose they are obliged to maintain that the two letters addressed by that Pope to Sergius of Constantinople were really written *ex cathedrâ*, and that they present all the characters of dogmatic letters. Mr. Renouf, in his recent pamphlet, has done nothing but follow in their steps, reproducing all the stock arguments, and adding nothing of his own but the extraordinary boldness with which he puts forward their historical mistakes as indisputable facts, and their erroneous principles as certain and unimpeachable truths. His arguments have already been answered in the *Dublin Review* and the *Westminster Gazette*. Before proceeding to give our own remarks upon them, it will be well to state summarily the marks which characterise a papal document as *ex cathedrâ*, in a matter of faith.

It cannot be doubted that *cathedra* (θρόνος) means the papal authentic magisterium; so that a Pope teaches *ex cathedrâ* when he teaches authentically in the Universal Church in virtue of that divine power by which he is appointed œcumenical doctor and teacher. But when he thus teaches the Universal Church and points out some doctrine as a rule of faith, he cannot leave it at the same time as an open question, as a matter on which judgment has yet to be pronounced, or on which silence is to be held till a definitive sentence be issued. He must demand interior assent and exterior submission to his dogmatic decree, since he speaks as the organ of God in this world and as infallible interpreter of God's revelations. Therefore, when in any letter a Pope shows no such intention of imposing on the Universal Church such a strict obligation of absolute assent to his decisions of faith, his letter cannot be said to be *ex cathedrâ*, nor dogmatic in the proper meaning of the word. Consequently, in order that a papal utterance may have the character of a teaching *ex cathedrâ*, it is requisite first, not only that it should treat of a question of faith, but that it should propose a doctrine to be believed or condemned; secondly, that the Pope should show the intention of teaching as Pope, and of enforcing his doctrinal decrees on the Universal Church. If either of these two qualities be wanting, the letter cannot be said to contain any teaching *ex cathedrâ*. This is what all Catholics, without exception, admit as necessary and essential to an infallible document issued by papal authority. But according to the discipline and practice of the Church in ancient times, which was preserved for many centuries, there are some solemnities which were ordinarily observed when dogmatic constitutions were despatched by Roman Pontiffs. They were previously read and examined in the synod of the Bishops of Italy, with whom the prelates of neighbouring provinces were sometimes associated, or in the assembly of the clergy of the Roman Church.[25] Again, they were sent to the Patriarchs, or even to the Primates and Metropolitans, that they might be

[25] The place of these meetings was later supplied by the consistories of the Cardinals where the Popes read their utterances destined to be despatched to the Universal Church.

everywhere known and obeyed. Finally, the signatures of all the Bishops were often required to those papal constitutions, to show their submission and adhesion to them. We do not now mean to spend time in demonstrating these points of ancient ecclesiastical discipline; they will be found proved beyond all question in the learned works of Coustant,[20] Thomassin,[27] and Cardinal Orsi.[28] A few remarks, however, will be useful as throwing light on the matter immediately in hand. First, it must be distinctly understood that we do not maintain the absolute necessity of the above-mentioned characters, as if no papal utterance of that age could be *ex cathedrâ* if any one of these marks were wanting; but we maintain affirmatively, that papal utterances bearing all these characters were to be regarded as certainly issued *ex cathedrâ*; and negatively, that no papal decree could be considered at that time as *ex cathedrâ* if wanting in all and each of those characters. Thus, although we believe that the famous letter of St. Leo to Flavian, Patriarch of Constantinople, had been read in a Roman synod,[29]

[20] Coustant. Epist. RR. Pont. præfatio, n. 33 seq. pp. xxxi. seq.

[27] Thomassinus, Dissertationes in Conc. Gen. Diss. xx. in vi. Syn. § viii. seq. p. 460.

[28] Orsi, de Romani Pontificis Auctoritate, t. i. l. i. c. xxii. art. ii. § i. p. 168 seq. ed. Romæ, 1771.

[29] Although neither in the Libellus Synodicus, nor in any other document of the time, is there clear mention made of St. Leo's letter having been read in an especial meeting of Bishops at Rome, nevertheless it is known that at that age it was customary for the Bishops of several provinces to meet in Rome every year in the beginning of October to hold a synod for the affairs of the Church: so that we cannot doubt that Pope Leo had then treated of the heresy of Eutyches, of the two councils of Constantinople

still we do not consider it necessary to prove this point against the author of the *Defensio Declarationis Cleri Gallicani*,[30] because this at least is certain, that it was forwarded to all the Patriarchs and Bishops of both Churches, Latin and Greek, and signed by them as a symbol of faith, before any dogmatic decree had been agreed on by the Council of Chalcedon.[31] The same writer adduces two other alleged exceptions to the synodical character of papal utterances *ex cathedrâ*, namely, the letters of Innocent I. to the African councils, and that of St. Celestine to St. Cyril. As to these, we will remark briefly, that the letter of St. Celestine to St. Cyril, in which a definitive sentence was pronounced against Nestorius, was truly a synodical letter,[32] as was that of Siricius against Jovinian,[33] and that of Zosimus against Celestius.[34] Moreover, we say that the letters of Innocent I. to the Councils

---

held by Flavian against it, and of his dogmatic letter destined to be read in the Synod of Ephesus; especially as, after the miserable end of that council we see no less than three Roman synods held by Leo against Dioscorus, and in the cause of the Eutychians. (Labbe, t. iv. pp. 747-751.) Besides which, St. Leo's letter to Flavian, read in the second session of the Council of Chalcedon (Labbe, l. c. p. 1214), bears the title of *Epistola Synodica*, and in the Greek translation of 'Ἐπιστολὴ ἐγκύκλιος ἤγουν συνοδική. Indeed, according to the practice of that time, the circular letters of the Pope were always considered to be written in council.

[30] Defensio Decl. Cleri Gallicani, t. ii. l xii. cap. xxii. p. 185. ed. Basileæ.

[31] Vide Ballerini Admonitionem in Epist. xxviii. S. Leonis. (S. Leonis Ep. t. i. p. 794.)

[32] Labbe, t. iii. p. 551 seq.

[33] Siricius, Epist. vii. (Constant. p. 663 seq.)

[34] Zosimus, Tractatoria. (Constant. p. 994 seq.)

of Carthage and of Milevis,[35] did not need to be read and examined in a Roman synod, since they were written merely in confirmation of decrees already discussed and examined in a synodical manner, to which nothing was wanting but the confirmation of the supreme authority in the Church. Apostolical letters such as these were not usually brought before the Roman synod, in the manner which was practised when the matter was such as needed examination and discussion, before the supreme infallible sentence of the Pope was pronounced.

But whatever exception there may be to the synodical character of papal utterances *ex cathedrâ* from the second down to the sixth century, it is most certain that in the age of Pope Honorius such was the custom and the practice of the Church, not only at Rome, but also in other patriarchal and metropolitan churches. The *Liber Synodicus* mentions no less than thirteen synods, some Catholic and some heretical, which were held in the cause of the Monothelites; so that all the utterances published at that time either in condemnation or defence of Monothelism were synodical. Such were the apostolic decrees of Pope Severinus, the successor of Honorius,[36] of John IV., of Theodorus, of Martin, of Agatho,[37] not to speak of the synodical letters of Patriarchs and Primates issued about that time upon

---

[35] Constant. Epist. RR. PP. p. 887 seq. p. 895 seq.
[36] V. Conc. Lat. Secr. iii. (Labbe, t. vii. p. 215). Pagi, Crit. in Annal. Baronii, t. ii. an. 639, n. v. p. 818. Antwerpia, 1727.
[37] Liber Synodicus. (Labbe, t. vii. p. 1443 seq.)

the same subject. Now we distinctly assert that both the letters of Pope Honorius, read in the twelfth and thirteenth sessions of the Sixth Council, were utterly devoid, not only of the synodical character, but also of all the other marks which have been mentioned as required by the discipline of the time to constitute a papal utterance *ex cathedrâ*. Moreover they are wanting in the two other internal characters which must be found expressly or by implication in every papal constitution in a matter of faith. Mr. Renouf, with his usual boldness of language, calls it "a mockery to consider the Pope's solemn public and most earnest reply to the eastern Patriarchs otherwise than as *ex cathedrâ*."[38] But he should have known that Catholic apologists of Honorius, including even those who accuse him of error, utterly deny that his reply was solemn and public; and much more do we deny that his letters concerned any matter properly of faith. Mr. Renouf reasons in this manner: "Pope Honorius was officially consulted by the Patriarchs of Constantinople and Jerusalem merely because he was Pope, and on a question of faith which all parties considered of supreme importance;" and from this he concludes that the reply must have been solemn and public, *ex cathedrâ* and *de fide*. We answer, first, that it does not follow; and next, is the antecedent altogether true? We think not; for he seems to represent not only Sophronius of Jerusalem, but Sergius himself, as applying to the Pope for a definitive decision on the subject

[38] Condemnation of Pope Honorius, p. 21.

of the existence of two operations or of one in Christ. Now we altogether deny that the letter of Sergius contained such an application. The Patriarch of Constantinople was too crafty and skilful to lay bare his own heretical mind; much less would he have disclosed to the Pope the true nature of the controversy, that he might pronounce a final judgment upon it.

Sergius was aware that in the Latin Church, and especially at Rome, the dogma of the Incarnation was perfectly understood in its full meaning and extent. He knew well the dogmatic letter of Pope Leo, in which the doctrine of the two operations in Christ had been sufficiently stated, and he could not be ignorant that this letter had been everywhere studied and regarded as a complete exposition of faith in the matter. It would have been foolish to call at once for a definitive sentence from the very See which had issued the dogmatic letter on the Incarnation of Christ; and yet more foolish and imprudent to brave the decision of Rome, at a moment when Sophronius, the most energetic defender of the two operations in Christ, had been raised to the patriarchal See of Jerusalem. The most elementary rules of prudence would have suggested to him to reconnoitre his ground before making the final assault. In a moment of such danger the hypocritical heresiarch was obliged to have recourse to half measures, which might have some appearance of plausibility and prudence, rather than adopt at once an extreme policy, which, all things considered, could have no chance of success. With all his perversity, Sergius was not wanting in common sense, and in this respect an injustice has been done to him by the author of the *Condemnation of Pope Honorius*. He did not hesitate to adopt the line of action which prudence dictated. His letter to Honorius may be read in the acts of the twelfth session of the sixth General Council, and will be found to bear no other construction than that which we have put upon it.

In this letter Sergius used every artifice which his craft could suggest as likely to mislead the Pope and to gain him over to his side. He described, in exaggerated terms, the return of the Monophysites to the Catholic Church: he attributed to them more sincerity than was their due; and his estimate of their numbers was cunningly exaggerated. He made a show of detesting the errors of the Monophysites, and he spoke of their writers as hateful to God: Εὐτυχοῦς καὶ Διοσκόρου, Σιβήρου κ.τ.λ. θεοστυγῶν.[39] On the other hand, he showed the highest respect for the "divinely-speaking" Pope Leo (θεσπισίου Λέοντος), and for the Fathers of the holy Council of Chalcedon, whose names were solemnly inserted in the diptychs in the celebration of the divine mysteries by the reconciled heretics.[40] He described as imprudent the opposition to the seven articles of the act of concord arranged with the Theodosians by the Patriarch Cyrus, which was raised by Sophro-

---

[39] Epistola Sergii ad Honorium Papam. In act. xii. conc. vi. (Labbe, t. vii. p. 953.)
[40] (Ib. p. 956.)

nius, then a monk of Alexandria, on account of a single word on the subject of one operation in Christ, which word had, however, the sanction of several Fathers. He added, that it would be harsh and cruel to drive millions of souls into heresy and perdition for the sake of one expression: that in similar contingencies the Fathers had often followed an *economy* pleasing to God (διαφόροις οἰκονομίαις) for the salvation of many souls. He observed, however, that, although the controversy was merely verbal, it had nevertheless much exasperated men's minds, so that there was reason to fear the rise of a new party openly heretical: on these accounts he judged that it would be a prudent economy to impose silence on both the contending parties, requiring that none should make mention either of one or two operations in Christ, but that all should hold and defend the known doctrine which the Fathers had delivered. He said that, on the one hand, the expression "one operation and will" was offensive to many, to whom it seemed to destroy the distinction of the two natures in Christ: on the other hand, the expression "two operations and wills" would convey to the minds of many the idea of two contrary and conflicting wills coexisting in Christ. The Patriarch, moreover, informed the Pope that Sophronius himself had pledged his word to observe this economy, and that even the Emperor Heraclius had adopted his advice.[41] He concluded with the

[41] Epistola Sergii ad Honorium Papam. In act. xii. conc. vi. (Labbe, t. vii. pp. 957-959.)

request that the Pontiff would read the account and explanation he had given, and would let him know his thoughts upon the matter.[42]

It is true that Sergius, here and there, in his letter, tried to insinuate his pernicious doctrine of one operation and will in Christ; but first he did it very cautiously, either, as we have said before, by assuming in its explanation[43] a Catholic doctrine, or by endeavouring to reconcile his heretical views with the doctrine set forth by St. Leo; and moreover, he affected to speak of the point merely in passing and historically, without making it the principal object of his application to the Pope. His apparent purpose in writing is to gain the sanction of Honorius for the economy of silence on the subject of one or two operations in Christ, and for enforcing the same conduct on the Patriarch Sophronius; whilst at the same time he does not miss the favourable opportunity for sounding the mind of the Pontiff on the subject of the operations in Christ. The Pope, in his letter to Sergius, answered precisely the question asked by the Patriarch. Mr. Renouf asserts that he "gave his unqualified approbation to the doctrine of Sergius as contained in the letters written by the Patriarch to himself and to Sophronius."[44] But we hope to show in the next section that the doctrine set forth by Honorius in the first

---

[42] τὰ περὶ τούτων ὑμῖν δοκοῦντα σημᾶναι. Epistola Sergii ad Honorium Papam. In act. xii. conc. vi. (Labbe, t. vii. p. 960.)

[43] See n. 1. p. 14.

[44] The Condemnation of Pope Honorius, p. 21.

as well as the second letter to Sergius has nothing to do with the Monothelite dogma contained in the letter of the latter. For the present we maintain only that in neither of the two letters did Honorius give the least hint that he intended to impose any belief of doctrine *ex cathedrâ*: his first letter answers the purpose of the Patriarch, and authorises his economy of silence on the subject of the operations of Christ. In the opening of his letter he praises Sergius for having stopped the rise of a new word which was liable to be misunderstood and to create scandal among the simple.[45] In concluding, he exhorts Sergius to preach the orthodox doctrine of unity of Person in Christ, and of two distinct natures by which He performs the divine and human actions, but to abstain from the new expression of one or two operations.[46] In the other letter to the same Patriarch the Pope expressly declares that it is not necessary to define one or two operations in Christ, but rather to suppress the scandal of the new and subtle invention.[47] He assures the Patriarch

[45] "Laudamus novitatem vocabuli auferentem, quod posset scandalum simplicibus generare." Epist. Honorii ad Sergium. In act. xii. conc. vi. (Labbe, l. c. p. 962.)

[46] "Hortantes vos, ut, unius vel geminæ novæ vocis inductum operationis vocabulum aufugientes, unum nobiscum Dominum Jesum Christum filium Dei vivi, Deum verissimum in duabus naturis operatum divinitus atque humanitus fide orthodoxa et unitate Catholica prædicetis." (Ib. p. 966.)

[47] "Auferentes ergo, sicut diximus, scandalum novellæ adinventionis, non nos oportet unam vel duas operationes definientes prædicare." Ib. In act. xiii. conc. vi. (Labbe, l. c. p. 1003.)

that he had written to Cyrus and to Sophronius, urging them to avoid the expression of a single or twofold operation. As to the legates sent to him by Sophronius, he says that he urgently recommended to them the use of the same economy, and that they had promised that their Patriarch would willingly refrain from the expression "two operations," if Cyrus of Alexandria would no longer speak of one operation.[48]

Now in neither of these letters does Honorius show any intention but that of approving of the economy of silence which Sergius proposed, as the best means to save the Church from the misfortune of a new outbreak of that sectarian violence which had been so lately allayed; and this economy he inculcates only by way of suggestion and exhortation. His first letter concludes with an exhortation which sums up what he had explained in the course of it, and which contains the expression of his will. In the second letter he again suggests and insinuates to Sergius (*hoc quidem fraternitati vestræ insinuandum prævidimus*) the same principles as he had inculcated on Cyrus and Sophronius by letter. It is impossible to construe this form of writing into an utterance *ex cathedrâ*. The Pope manifests no intention whatever of imposing any rigorous obligation, of defining any doctrine, of requiring any interior consent, in virtue of his apostolic divine authority. The only purpose to which he points is

[48] Epist. Honorii ad Sergium. In act. xiii. conc. vi. (Labbe, L c. p. 1003.)

that of approving and suggesting the economy of silence by exhortation and persuasion. But Mr. Renouf persists in seeing language *ex cathedrâ* in the authoritative manner in which the Pope addresses Sergius in the second letter, and he quotes as follows: "We have decided" (συνίδομεν, a word of supreme authority in the Greek of the period) "to make manifest by the present letters to your most holy fraternity," &c.; and further on, "and these things we have decided (συνίδομεν) to make known to your most blessed fraternity," &c.[49] First, then, we do not see why Mr. Renouf puts so great stress on the word συνίδομεν, which, even if it had been an exact translation of the original Latin text of the letter of Honorius, would mean no more than *censemus*, and not precisely "we have decided." In the thirteenth session of the sixth synod sentence was pronounced against Sergius, Cyrus, Theodorus, and Pyrrhus, and the words used are ἐκρίναμεν and ὁρίζομεν. These are really words of great authority; and of the two translators of the Council one rendered them by *judicavimus et definimus*,[50] the other by *statuimus et decernimus*.[51] A few lines further on, when speaking of Honorius, the Council used the word συνίδομεν, which the two interpreters rendered, one *prævidimus*, the other *censemus;* and in rendering the passage of Hono-

[49] The Condemnation of Pope Honorius, p. 22.
[50] Labbe, l. c. pp. 977-978.
[51] Ex vetusto codice Bibl. Paris. Soc. Jesu. (Labbe, l. c. p. 1281.)

rius, quoted by Mr. Renouf, they use respectively the same words; and they correctly express the true meaning of the word in question.[52] Again, why does Mr. Renouf insist that Pope Honorius, in his letters to Sergius, spoke with supreme authority as Pope? No defender of papal infallibility would deny this, but it cannot be inferred from the admission that the document was a teaching *ex cathedrâ*; yet he seems to think that no less must follow. In order to impose silence upon contending Patriarchs, the Pope must of course exercise his pontifical authority, and communicate his determination by official letters. But it is not true that the Pope, every time he exercises his pontifical authority in a particular case, teaches *ex cathedrâ*, and exercises his authentic infallible magisterium. Mr. Renouf professes himself a Catholic, and does not reject the papal supremacy, although he may deny the infallibility of the Pope's teaching; and he cannot fail to be acquainted with the manifold character of the action adopted by the Pope in the general government of the Church. He ought to remember that if "the Pope is consulted merely because he is Pope," it does not follow that all his utterances are necessarily *ex cathedrâ*. But the Pope was called upon, insists Mr. Renouf,[53] "by no less than the Patriarchs of Constantinople and Jerusalem to give his judgment on a question of faith which all parties considered as of supreme importance." As to the Patriarch Sergius, we have

[52] See the Lexicons under the words συντίθει and συνοράω.
[53] The Condemnation of Pope Honorius, p. 19.

seen that the Pope was called upon in a question of faith, but not to give his judgment on it. With regard to the Patriarch Sophronius, it is true that he sent his legates to Honorius, begging him to pronounce his final judgment upon the Monothelite controversy. This is clearly proved by the synodical letter of Sophronius to Sergius, which letter was communicated to the Pope. But we have already remarked that Honorius not only abstained from giving any definitive sentence in the matter, but he persuaded the representatives of the Patriarch of Jerusalem to observe the economy of silence on the subject of the two wills and operations, as in another letter to the Patriarch of Alexandria he had enjoined abstinence from the expression, "one operation in Christ." In doing this he committed a fault which we are not here called upon to characterise; but unquestionably he could not have pronounced any sentence *ex cathedrâ* on the question of Christ's two wills and operations at the very time when he was aiming at quieting the controversy by an economy of silence.

Again, the letters of Pope Honorius to Sergius cannot be *ex cathedrâ*, because they are devoid of all those characters which at that period denoted papal utterances of the kind. Mr. Renouf affects to ignore this important point on which the apologists of Pope Honorius so justly insist. It is undeniable that these letters, be their doctrine what it may, were not synodical. No proof whatever can be adduced tending to show that they had that character.

In the *Liber Synodalis*, and other documents of the time, all the synods are mentioned to which any of the successors of Honorius submitted their *ex cathedrâ* decisions; but no mention is made of anything of that kind concerning the letters of Honorius. In the *Liber Diurnus* three formulas of faith are inserted, which the successors of Honorius were accustomed to subscribe. They profess in them to hold and observe all the constitutions of their predecessors which were synodically decreed.[54] Consequently they show indirectly that Honorius had decreed nothing synodically in favour of the Monothelites; especially as in the second of these formulas of faith they openly reject and condemn the epistles of Honorius, as favourable to those sectarians who 'obstinately defended the heretical dogma against the truth of the faith synodically declared and denounced.'[55] Therefore, according to these professions of faith, what is synodically settled belongs to the truth of faith, and cannot be rejected, much less condemned. Since, then, the letters of Honorius were rejected and condemned in those professions, they cannot have had the synodical character. On this account in the sixth council they are never called synodical, although the synod gives that epithet to the letter of Sophronius,[56] and to the letters of Thomas, John, and

[54] Liber Diurnus RR. PP. cum notis Garnerii, c. ii. tit. ix. Professio ii. (In Migne, PP. LL. t. cv. pp. 53-54.)
[55] "Simulque et hos qui hæretica dogmata contra veritatem fidei synodaliter declaratam atque prædicatam pertinaciter defendobant." (Ib. p. 52.)
[56] Act. xi. (Labbe, l. c. pp. 881-884.)

Constantine, Patriarchs of Constantinople.[87] Nay, even when the letters of Honorius are mentioned in conjunction with the synodical letters of Sophronius, the former are distinguished from the latter by the absence of any such qualification;[58] and this omission affords a strong argument in favour of what we assert.[59] Besides this, the letters in question were wanting in the most essential character of a papal utterance *ex cathedrâ*, that they were not intended for the instruction of the whole Church. Far from this, they were not even destined for circulation among all the Bishops of either East or West; still less were the Bishops required to sign them. Mr. Renouf ought to have known the facts to which we refer; but he has passed them over in his pamphlet without the least notice. Again, it is a fact that no record whatever exists from which we learn that the letters of Honorius were communicated to the Oriental Bishops. Sergius, who was principally interested in the matter, did not put them in circulation, nor did he even mention them in the *Ecthesis*, which was his own composition. It seems that the Patriarch was anxious rather to withdraw them from view and bury them in the archives of the Church of Constantinople, where they were found in their Latin autograph, accompanied by a Greek version, at the time of the Sixth Council.[60] Pyrrhus also, the suc-

[57] Act. xiii. (Labbe, l. c. p. 1000.)
[58] Act. xii. (Labbe, l. c. p. 969.)
[59] See Card. Orsi, de Romani Pontificis Auctoritate, t. i. p. i. l. i. c. xxii. art. ii. § ii. p. 190 seq. ed. Romæ, 1771.
[60] Conc. vi. act. xii. xiii. (Labbe, l. c. pp. 969-1001.)

cessor of Sergius, does not appear to have published them, but only to have put in circulation a small extract from the first of them, which admitted of being misconstrued in an heretical meaning.

In the Lateran Council no mention was made of these letters, either by Stephen of Dora or by the Greek monks in their "libelli," presented to that synod against the errors of Sergius and his followers. The very "Typus" of Constans, whilst it forbade all further controversy on the subject of one will or two wills, did not even remotely allude to these letters of Honorius. Moreover it is certain that in the West they remained unknown for a long time, until Pyrrhus, successor of Sergius in the See of Constantinople, circulated an extract from them in the West with the view of persuading the Western Prelates that Honorius had been a Monothelite.[61] Certainly in no one of the many synods held in Rome and in Africa after the death of Honorius was any mention whatever made of them. Even, then, if all internal proof were wanting, the very fact that the letters are without any of the characters which in that period distinguish all papal utterances *ex cathedrâ*, affords of itself conclusive proof that they were not written by Honorius with the intention of imposing doctrine to be believed, and that they were not received by the Patriarchs to whom they were addressed as containing an authoritative exposition.[62]

[61] Vide Joannis IV. Apologia pro Honorio Papa. (Labbe, t. vi. p. 1511.)

[62] See Muzzarelli, de Auctoritate Rom. Pontif. in Conc. Gen. t. ii. c. x. § ii. p. 181 seq. Gandavi.

A striking confirmation of this fact is found in the mission intrusted by Sophronius, Patriarch of Jerusalem, to Stephen, Bishop of Dora, one of his principal suffragans.

The Patriarch Sophronius, one of the most distinguished men of the age for his learning, prudence, zeal, and virtue, fully understood the bearing of the heresy in all its points. He knew perfectly well what was the state of the East at that period, and the rapid growth and spread of error since the time when the economy of silence was adopted on the double operation in Christ. But the Arabs were just then making their victorious advance through Palestine, with the prospect of besieging and capturing the Holy City itself; and at such a crisis the Patriarch could not quit his see and undertake the long journey to Rome, in order to lay before the Pope the real state of the Monothelite controversy, and obtain his final condemnation of the heresy. He was forced, therefore, to intrust this important mission to a legate; and he fixed on Stephen, Bishop of Dora, for the purpose. Sophronius used every means to insure the faithful execution of his commission, taking Stephen with him to the very scene of our Lord's crucifixion, and there binding him by a solemn oath to repair with all speed to Rome, and never to rest until he had secured a final condemnation of Monothelism. He pictured before the eyes of the holy Bishop the crucifixion and the last judgment, with the object of powerfully moving him to bring to the most successful issue possible a legation the responsibility of which was the heaviest that had ever been laid upon him.[63]

Before we proceed to consider the bearings of this fact upon the subject before us, we must discuss some previous questions which arise out of Mr. Renouf's remarks upon the matter. He mentions the fact referred to,[64] but, with his ordinary looseness of assertion, commits two great mistakes, which he might have avoided by the study of the Church History of his friend Dr. Döllinger.[65] First, he confounds the two embassies sent by Sophronius to the Pope; and next, he supposes that the second, of which Stephen of Dora was the head, reached Rome in the lifetime of Pope Honorius, so that he treats the second letter of Honorius as belonging to it.

We cannot be surprised at some of the errors into which Mr. Renouf has fallen, for they are common to most writers upon the subject; but it is strange that one who professes to have "thoroughly mastered" the question should speak of the embassy of Stephen of Dora as corroborating the view which he has taken of the conduct of Honorius, and yet betray no consciousness that the historical statements on which he relies were called in question and rejected even by Fleury,[66] and have been tri-

---

[63] Libellus Stephani Dorensis Episcopi, in Conc. Lat. Secr. ii. (Labbe, t. vii. p. 108.)

[64] The Condemnation of Pope Honorius, pp. 20-21.

[65] History of the Church, translated by Dr. Cox, vol. ii. sect. vii. p. 197 seq. London, 1840.

[66] Fleury himself, who is no ultramontane, had long ago represented these facts in the same sense. See Hist. Eccl. l. xxxviii. § vi.-viii. t. viii. p. 367 seq. Paris, 1751.

umphantly refuted by Orsi[67] and others. The fact is, that although Stephen of Dora received his mission from Sophronius whilst Honorius yet ruled the Church, he did not reach Rome before the death of the Pope; for as he himself informs us in his *Libellus*, when the Monothelites got information of the nature of his legation to Rome they sent orders to all the provinces that he should be taken prisoner; and he was accordingly captured, put in chains, and detained in a prison until it pleased God to deliver him from the hands of his persecutors. Then, mindful of his oath and the orders, the prayers, and the tears of Sophronius and of all the Catholic Bishops of the East, he hastened without delay to Rome.[68] He does not speak in detail of the fulfilment of his mission, but he says enough of it to convince us that he executed his commission, and laid the matter before the successors of Honorius, not before Honorius himself. For after having mentioned that, subsequently to his liberation from the hands of his enemies, he made haste to reach the Apostolic See, he continues: "Neither did God disregard the prayer and tears which were offered to Him by His faithful servants, but He stirred up your predecessors in the Apostolic See to be vigorous in exhorting and amending the aforesaid persons [the heads of the Monothelites], although they wholly failed in overcoming the obstinacy of the heretics."[69]

[67] De R. P. Auctoritate, l. c. § iv. p. 200 seq.
[68] Libellus Stephani Dorensis, in Secr. ii. Conc. Lat. (Labbe, t. vii. p. 107.)
[69] l. c. οὐ παρεῖδεν ὁ Θεὸς τὴν δέησιν τῶν οἰκετῶν αὐτοῦ μετὰ δακρύων

These words cannot possibly refer to Honorius, and must refer to his immediate successors; for of the former it could not be said that by his economy of silence he had tried to amend the leaders of the heresy, and bring them to a better sense. It follows, that the silence which Stephen observes in his *Libellus* about his reception by Honorius, is not, as Mr. Renouf supposes, to be explained partly by the economy practised by the Lateran Fathers with reference to this Pope, and partly by the fact that he himself had betrayed the trust confided to him by Sophronius.[70] When once it is shown that Stephen of Dora did not reach Rome before the death of Honorius, the two reasons pointed out by Mr. Renouf as an explanation of the Bishop's silence about Honorius fall to the ground. Even Mr. Renouf allows that the embassy of Stephen of Dora was a very solemn one. But it was the custom of that age and of all antiquity, that every prelate, and especially every Patriarch, on entering upon his office should send a synodical letter with an ordinary legation to Rome and to all the patriarchates, to testify his orthodox faith and Catholic communion. On this account Sophronius despatched Leontius the deacon and Polyeuctes to Sergius with his synodical letter, which was read in the eleventh session

---

προσαγομένη, ἀλλ' ἤγειρε μὲν οὐ μετρίως τοὺς προλαβόντας ἀποστολικοὺς ἀρχιερίας, εἰς παραίνεσιν, ἅμα καὶ διαμαρτυρίαν τῶν εἰρημένων ἀνδρῶν, εἰ καὶ μηδαμῶς τούτους ἱμάλαξαν.

[70] Condemnation of Pope Honorius, p. 21.

of the Sixth Synod.[71] He sent at the same time, or perhaps a little before, the very same synodical letter to Pope Honorius by the hands of other legates.[72]

This legation, however, could not be the same which Stephen of Dora mentions in his *Libellus*. The former was sent when the Patriarch of Jerusalem still entertained hopes of bringing round Sergius, Cyrus, and the others; therefore, in his synodical letter to Sergius, he speaks in high terms of that Patriarch, and willingly submits to his advice and correction.[73] Stephen must have alluded to this when he spoke of the endeavours made by the holy Patriarch "to recall to the true faith of their ancestors the authors of the new error."[74] But when Sophronius sent Stephen of Dora to Rome he had lost all hope of ameliorating the state of things. His zealous and holy efforts, as Stephen himself tells us, were not able to procure the conversion of Sergius and Cyrus with their faction, but only aroused against him an anger which displayed itself in merciless persecution. It was then that the holy Patriarch saw that no other means was left to counteract the evils of the new heresy than to apply to that see

---

[71] See the synodical letter in the VI. Council, sess. xi. (Labbo, t. vii. p. 884-932.) Ib. p. 929, the names of the two Legates are mentioned.

[72] In several ms. codices this synodical letter is addressed to Pope Honorius. Fleury himself asserts this in his Hist. Eccl. l. xxxviii. § vi. p. 367, t. viii.

[73] L. c. p. 928.

[74] Libellus Stephani Dorensis (l. c. p. 108).

where the foundations of the orthodox doctrine are laid, and to call upon him who has been appointed by Christ to feed His flock.[75] The two legations to Rome are, therefore, evidently distinct.[76] The economy of silence must have been suggested by Honorius to the representatives of Sophronius at the time of the first legation, and accepted by them in the name of the Patriarch, because at that time he still cherished some hope of a pacific settlement of the controversy, and of the triumph of the Catholic doctrine. That this was the state of the case is the more evident, since, as we have seen above, the legation of Stephen of Dora did not reach Rome before the death of Honorius. Consequently we must conclude, first, that in despatching his second embassy to Honorius, Sophronius acknowledged that the Pope had not in either of his letters to Sergius manifested the slightest intention of proposing any supreme definition *ex cathedrâ*, because he so earnestly recommended to Stephen of Dora not to desist from his endeavours until he had obtained the final judgment from the "apostolical divine wisdom;" and secondly, that nowithstanding the two letters of Honorius and the economy of silence adopted by him, Sophronius, when sending Stephen to that Pope, solemnly professed the doctrine of papal infallibility; for what

[75] Libellus Stephani Dorensis (l. c. p. 108).
[76] We regret that Pagi, notwithstanding his penetrating critical acumen, has fallen into the same mistake of not distinguishing the two legations of Sophronius to Honorius (see Critica in Annales Baronii, an. 633, n. xi. t. ii. p. 802). But at the time in which he lived no doubts had been raised concerning this erroneous view.

else can be the meaning of the expression that "the foundations of orthodox doctrine rest on the Apostolic See"?[77] What too can be the meaning of a "judgment from the apostolic divine wisdom," but a guarantee of the complete overthrow of the new errors?[78] We may at least call upon the opponents of papal infallibility to give some explanation of these expressions that shall not be destructive of their theory. And finally we may remark, that Sophronius clearly did not look upon Honorius as an adherent of the heretical faction.

Another remark of Mr. Renouf's seems to us to betray a great want of theological knowledge. "It will, however, be observed," he says, "that St. Sophronius does not simply submit his opinion to the judgment of the Pope: he lays down the truth, which he wishes to be confirmed by the Pope, but he will not swerve from it."[79] We do not know to what passage the words cited refer. From the quotation we should think that they refer to the words addressed by Sophronius to Stephen of Dora when intrusting him with the legation to the Apostolic See; but we have read them over again and again without finding any hint of the sense suggested by Mr. Renouf, or of the meaning of Mr. Renouf's paraphrase. "Sophronius," he says, "lays down the truth,

[77] ταχέως οὖν ἀπὸ περάτων εἰς πέρατα διῆλθι, μέχρις ἂν εἰς τὸν ἀποστολικὸν καταντήσειας θρόνον, ἴνθα τῶν εὐσεβῶν δογμάτων εἰσὶν αἱ κρηπῖδες. l. c. p. 108.

[78] ἐξ ἀποστολ.πῆς θεοσοφίας εἰς νῖκος τὴν κρίσιν . . . καὶ τῶν ἐπεισάκτων δογμάτων, τελείαν ποιήσονται κανονικῶς τὴν κατάργησιν. L. c.

[79] The Condemnation of Pope Honorius, p. 20, in the note.

which he wishes to be confirmed by the Pope, but he will not swerve from it." Is it to be expected that Sophronius should declare himself ready to swerve from the truth? And did he think that the Pope teaching *ex cathedrâ* would propose anything to be believed except the *truth*?

Again, there are two kinds of cases in which doctrines may be said to be defined by the Pope. One regards doctrines which are not contained in a clear manner in the universal magisterium of the Church, and which are disputed on both sides, as was for several centuries the doctrine of the Immaculate Conception, with many others. The second concerns doctrines clearly revealed and universally believed as dogmas of faith, although they have never been defined explicitly and under anathema by the authentic magisterium. Such was the doctrine of the consubstantiality of the Divine Word, and generally all the doctrines concerning the Incarnation. Now, the denial of a doctrine of the first class, before its infallible definition, does not constitute a sin of heresy: and if either of the two rival schools seek the supreme judgment of the Pope upon the question, it must be prepared to submit to that judgment, and be ready to reject the doctrine till then defended, and even to embrace the contrary teaching were it proposed by the Pope *ex cathedrâ*. But it is not so with doctrines of the other kind. A doctrine universally believed in the Church is infallibly *de fide*, the consent of the Church being equivalent to a formal and explicit definition. Therefore the Arians, the Nestorians, and the Eutychians were generally looked upon by the Catholics as heretics, even before any infallible sentence had been pronounced against them. In such cases, when a definition is required either from the Pope or from an Œcumenical Council, the request is made not properly for the instruction of the orthodox as to what they should believe in the matter, but only to crush and destroy error with the overwhelming authority of a supreme judgment. As to Catholics, those who, from ignorance or prejudice, have been led into error, are bound to wait for the infallible decree, and must hold themselves in readiness to submit unreservedly to the same; but others, who are fully acquainted with the teaching of the Church, must be steady in their adhesion to it while expecting that infallible decision which will finally confirm their faith. For the divine truth proposed in a decree of faith cannot possibly differ from the divine truth believed in the Universal Church. Consequently in such cases, when Catholics, already in possession of the Catholic truth, apply to the Pope or a General Council for a definition necessary to ensure the triumph of the faith over heresy, they should not harbour in their heart the smallest doubt concerning the doctrine laid before the Apostolic See. Much less should they say, as Mr. Renouf would have them do, that they will change their opinion if the Pope decides the other way! It is curious to observe the surprise of Mr. Renouf at not finding any such language in the confession of the faith presented by the orthodox abbots, priests, and monks to Pope Martin in the Lateran Council. Every student of theology would understand it; and we may well be amused at the arrogance of Mr. Renouf, who pretends to be judged by his *peers*—that is, by men who have studied the original sources, &c.—when he himself is guilty of theological and historical blunders of such magnitude.

The doctrine which Monothelism attacked was clearly proposed in the universal teaching of the Church, and generally admitted as a doctrine of faith. No definition in the matter would have altered in the least the substance of the Catholic dogma. Therefore, neither St. Sophronius, nor the abbots and monks mentioned by Mr. Renouf in his note, nor St. Maximus, could in any manner declare themselves ready to submit to any decision contrary to what had previously been preached in the Church. The case of Gilbert de la Poirée is explained on the same principle,[60] a knowledge of which would have spared Mr. Renouf the useless expenditure of words in his note.

---

[60] The errors of Gilbert de la Poirée regarded the simplicity of God, the unity of substance in the three divine Persons, the Incarnation of God in the Person of the Eternal Word; that is to say, the fundamental dogmas of the Catholic doctrine. Therefore the Bishops of France, who applied to Eugenius III. against that heretical Bishop of Poitiers, could not declare to the Pope that they were ready to change their faith. But that condition was to be admitted by Gilbert, who, in his Commentary on Boetius' work *De Trinitate*, had attacked the universal doctrine of the Church.

III.

Orthodox Doctrines contained in the two Letters of Pope Honorius to Sergius.

Two hundred years ago De Marca, a learned man of his time and a Gallican, left the following words in a manuscript dissertation, prepared by him as an apology for Pope Honorius, and which he had promised to his friend the erudite Labbe. "Quod ad Honorii doctrinam attinet, jam alii probaverunt eum prorsus aversum fuisse ab errore Monothelitarum, neque illis unquam consensisse; ut inutilis omnino futura sit mea opera, si velim hanc partem suscipere probandam."[1] Baluze, who put together the notes prepared by De Marca for the projected work which death prevented him from completing, does not question the correctness of his view. We may say, then, without fear of contradiction, that the view which represents Pope Honorius as having actually held Monothelite doctrine, has for nearly two centuries become almost exclusively the possession of Protestants and schismatics.[2] But unfortunately Cardinal de la Luzerne, in the early part of the present century, revived this false accusation in his work *La Déclaration de l'Assemblée du Clergé de France* A.D. 1682.[3] Later on, some professors in

[1] In vita Petri De Marca, scripta a Balutio, præmissa operibus De Marcæ, ed. Parisiis, 1663, p. 30.
[2] Anthimus also, Patriarch of Constantinople, in his encyclical letter of 1848, repeated again the stale calumny, and charged Pope Honorius with heresy.
[3] It appeared in Paris in the year 1820.

Germany took up the question of Pope Honorius, but unhappily in this case they did not apply those just principles of judgment with which some of their countrymen, Catholic and Protestant, have vindicated the memory of certain among the Popes, for centuries the victims of calumny and falsehood. Prejudice and passion interfered with their knowledge of facts and misled their judgments. Hefele, in his *History of the Councils*, believes that Honorius[4] expressed himself badly from inability to state his meaning correctly. But Dr. Döllinger, in his work on the *Papal Fables of the Middle Ages*,[5] tries by every means, even by the distortion of historical evidence, to prove that Pope Honorius was a rank Monothelite, and was condemned as such by the Sixth Synod. Mr. Renouf, who is so full of admiration of the German Positive School represented by Dr. Döllinger, in which the Gallican principles which have been exiled from France find refuge, thinks himself in perfect security by the side of such a champion. He seems also to believe that, supported by the authority of so great a name, he can speak very dogmatically, and set at defiance all the theologians and historians in the world who have ever attempted to clear Pope Honorius and his letters from the charge of heresy. He treats them all in the most contemptuous manner, saying that they betray

---

[4] Hefele, Conciliengeschichte, Dritter Band, § 296, p. 137, § 298, p. 150. Freiburg in Brisgau, 1858.

[5] Döllinger, Die Papst Fabeln des Mittelalters, vii. p. 133 seq. München, 1863.

an utter ignorance of the real nature of the controversy.⁶ Now, let us hear how Mr. Renouf reasons in the matter which he boastingly claims to have thoroughly mastered.⁷ "It is undeniable," he says, "that Honorius sided with Sergius against Sophronius, that he asserted his perfect agreement with the former, that he acknowledged but one will in Christ, and condemned as scandalous the assertion of 'two operations.'"⁸ Here let us pause. These three "undeniable propositions" of Mr. Renouf's are three gross blunders; and yet that gentleman, as he assures us, "has studied most carefully and conscientiously the original sources and entire literature of this and other portions of ecclesiastical history"!⁹ But, in order to see clearly that Pope Honorius did not in any manner teach the heresy of the Monothelites in his letters, we must recall to our mind the leading doctrine of that sect.

As we have shown at length in the first section of this pamphlet, the leading error of the Monothelites was identical with that of the Apollinarists and the Severians. They deprived the humanity of Christ of its natural operation (ἐνέργεια), and consequently of its will; they regarded it as an inactive instrument moved by the Divine Logos. Therefore their Monophytism (in the form given it by Severus) was not, as Mr. Renouf believes, "a mere logical

⁶ The Condemnation of Pope Honorius, p. 14.
⁷ See the letter which he addressed to the *Westminster Gazette* (20 June 1868).
⁸ The Condemnation of Pope Honorius, p. 14.
⁹ See the letter to the *Westminster Gazette*, quoted above.

consequence asserted by its adversaries;"[10] but it was the fundamental principle of the whole, and the source from which the system derives its very being.

The first question, then, to be examined is, whether Pope Honorius held any doctrine at all resembling the Monophytism of Severus, with its denial of the natural operation of Christ's humanity. It is undeniable that the doctrine of Honorius on this point is an explanation of St. Leo's doctrine in his dogmatic epistle, where he teaches the distinction of the two natures in Christ, and therefore the possession by each of a peculiar and intrinsic principle of operation, although under the government and dominion of the Word. St. Leo had said, " Agit utraque forma cum alterius communione quod proprium est; Verbo scilicet operante quod Verbi est, carne exsequente quod carnis est."[11] In these words the great Pope evidently lays down the doctrine of the two operations in Christ, in accordance with the distinction of His two natures, as well as that of the governing power of the Godhead by which the humanity was ruled.[12] The doctrine of the two operations is so clearly expressed in this passage that Cyrus of Phasis could not refrain from mentioning his anxiety on this score to Sergius;[13] and the *most honest* Pa-

[10] Condemnation of Pope Honorius, p. 18.
[11] Epist. xxviii. S. Leonis Papæ ad Flavianum, c. iv. (Op. t. i. ed. Ball. p. 819.)
[12] See the splendid exposition of this doctrine in St. Sophronius' synodical letter, read in the act. xi. of the Sixth Synod. (Labbe, t. vii. p. 906 seq.)
[13] Epist. Cyri Phasidis ad Sergium, in act. xiii. conc. vi. (Labbe, l. c. p. 984.)

triarch of Constantinople could not otherwise do away with his difficulty than by a solemn lie, by alleging, namely, that no one had ever said that Pope Leo, in the words quoted, asserted the doctrine of the two operations.[14] Moreover, as we have already said, Severus condemned St. Leo's dogmatic letter on account of its containing that doctrine. Now, what did Pope Honorius teach in his letters to Sergius, if not the identical doctrine set forth by Pope Leo in the foregoing passage and by Sophronius in his synodical letter?[15] He says, "Utrasque naturas in uno Christo unitate naturali copulatas cum alterius communione operantes atque operatrices confiteri debemus, et divinam quidem, quæ Dei sunt operantem, et humanam, quæ carnis sunt exequentem, non divise, neque confuse, aut convertibiliter Dei naturam in hominem et humanam in Dei conversam edicentes, sed naturarum differentias integras confitentes."[16] According, then, to the doctrine of Honorius, the human actions of Christ are to be attributed to the agency of human operation, not to that of the divine Word. But at the same time, the human nature, which of its own virtue operates what is peculiar to itself, is not separated from the divine nature, although distinct from it, because of

[14] Epist. Sergii ad Cyrum, in act. xii. conc. vi. (Labbe, l. c. p. 949.)
[15] Synodica Epistola Sophronii Patr. ad Sergium, in act. xi. conc. vi. (Labbe, l. c. p. 901 seq.)
[16] Epist. ii. Honorii Papæ ad Sergium, in act. xiii. conc. vi. (Labbe, l. c. p. 1003.) Mr. Renouf omits this passage in the long quotation from Honorius' letter in p. 22.

its hypostatical union with the Godhead. Sophronius, as we have remarked, professed this very identical dogma in his famous synodical letter. "As the two natures in Christ," he says, "keep each its own property in its entirety, so the one and the other operate what belongs to each, one with the communication of the other; the Word operates what is proper to the Word with the communication of the body, and the body executes what is of the body with the communication of the Word in the action itself. . . . . . Because they are not separated, whilst they act what is their own."[17] On the other hand, Sergius also, in his letter to Honorius, hypocritically referred to this passage of St. Leo; but he did so only in the hope of thereby disguising his error, in which, however, he was not altogether successful. His doctrine is seen to be Monothelite at a glance, and in opposition to that of Honorius and Sophronius. He expressed himself as follows: "We confess that the only-begotten Son of God, who is at the same time God and man, operates divine and human actions, and that all divine and human operation flows from the Incarnate Word of God without separation and division. For Leo, doorkeeper of heaven, taught us so," &c.[18] The Monothelite doctrine clearly

[17] Epist. Sophr. cit. (l. c. p. 901 seq.) ὥσπερ γὰρ ἐν Χριστῷ ἑκατέρα φυλάττει φύσις ἀνελλιπῶς τὴν ἑαυτῆς ἰδιότητα, οὕτω καὶ ἐνεργεῖ ἑκατέρα μορφὴ μετὰ τῆς θατέρου κοινωνίας τοῦθ᾽ ὅπερ ἴδιον ἔσχηκε, τοῦ μὲν λόγου κατεργαζομένου τοῦθ᾽, ὅπερ ἐστὶ τοῦ λόγου, μετὰ τῆς κοινωνίας δηλονότι τοῦ σώματος. τοῦ δὲ σώματος ἐκτελοῦντος ἅπερ ἐστὶ τοῦ σώματος, κοινωνοῦντος αὐτῷ δηλαδὴ τοῦ λόγου τῆς πράξεως . . . οὔτε γὰρ διῃρημένως ἐνήργουν τὰ ἴδια, κ. τ. λ.

[18] Epist. Sergii ad Honor. in act. xii. conc. vi. (Labbe, p. 960.)

appears from these words, however they may have
been intended to deceive. As long as Sergius had
said that "the Son of God, who is at the same time
God and man, operates divine and human actions,"
it could receive a Catholic explanation. But when
he adds that divine and human operation flows from
the Incarnate Word of God, he points manifestly to
the Monothelite doctrine of one divine operation in
Christ, flowing from the Word into His humanity,
which has not in itself any principle of action. And
this is the more clear, because he had a little before
declared that as the soul is the principle of movement
in our body, so is the Word in His humanity, which
is moved by Him alone.[19]

The Monothelite error is expressed here as clearly
as in the extracts of Theodorus of Pharan, quoted in
the first section. How, then, can it be said that
"Honorius sided with Sergius against Sophronius,"
when the doctrine of the former perfectly agrees with
that of Pope Leo, as well as with that of Sophronius,
and is in direct contradiction of the error of Sergius?
But what did Honorius mean when he expressed his
wish that they should refrain from the expression,
"one or two operations"? Did he mean that every-
body was to be free to reject the dogma of the two
operations in Christ? Mr. Renouf and his friends
look on this as undeniable. But those who read
Honorius' letter without prejudice, see that his
meaning is quite the contrary. Let us listen to
the Pope himself: "Non nos oportet unam vel duas

[19] Epist. Sergii ad Honorium, p. 957.

operationes definientes prædicare, sed pro unâ, quam quidam dicunt, operatione, oportet nos unum operatorem Christum Dominum in utrisque naturis veridice confiteri, et pro duabus operationibus, ablato geminæ operationis vocabulo, ipsas potius duas naturas, id est, divinitatis et carnis assumptæ, in unâ personâ Unigeniti Dei Patris, inconfuse, indivise, atque incontrovertibiliter nobiscum prædicare propria operantia."[20] Two fundamental doctrinal principles are here laid down by Honorius: the first is, that the Divine Word is the only leading primary principle (τὸ ἡγεμονικὸν) of all divine and human, free, or natural and necessary, actions of Christ; and therefore under this aspect the Word may be called the only source of operation. This doctrine was repeatedly inculcated in the synodical letter which Sophronius wrote against the Nestorian error. The second is, that, notwithstanding that hegemonic principle in Christ and the hypostatical union of His operations, both His natures preserved their integrity and their natural power of acting; so that, as the Pope says, we are to profess that both the natures operate in the unity of the divine Person. We have here the exact doctrine which the sixth synod proposed to the belief of the faithful in its definition of faith. But it is proper here to remark, that Honorius did not always use the word "operation" or "energy" in the sense of an internal principle of action implanted in our nature; but he employed it in his first letter to mean what the Greeks called ἐνέργημα,

[20] Epist. ii. Honorii ad Sergium, l. c. (Labbe, l. c. p. 1003.)

or the effect and external action itself. Thus he says, " Utrum autem propter opera divinitatis et humanitatis, una an geminæ operationes[21] debeant derivatæ dici vel intelligi, ad nos ista pertinere non debent," &c. ;[22] by which words he certainly did not mean the interior agency or power of the soul. Therefore he continues, " Nos non unam operationem vel duas Domini Jesu Christi ejusque Sanctum Spiritum sacris literis percepimus, sed multiformiter cognovimus operatum" (πολυτρόπως ἔγνωμεν αὐτὸν ἐνεργοῦντα); and further on : "Multis modis et ineffabilibus confiteri nos communione utriusque naturæ condecet operatum."[23] That multiplicity of actions in Christ evidently alludes to the external manifestation of the natural energy, not to the energy or agency itself. And this is the more manifest as Honorius quotes St. Paul's words,[24] in which the Apostle speaks of external acts (ἐνεργήματα), not of natural operation.[25] But "it is undeniable," insists Mr. Renouf, following in the footsteps of Dr. Döllinger,[26] "that Pope Honorius acknowledged but

[21] Epist. i. Honorii ad Sergium, in act. xii. synodi vi. (Labbe, l. c. p. 963.)

[22] Ib. l. c. p. 963.   [23] Ib. l. c. p. 966.   [24] 1 Cor. xii. 6.

[25] In the Greek text of the Epistle of Honorius instead of ἐνεργημάτων we read ἐνεργειῶν. This shows that among the Greeks the word ἐνέργεια was known to have both senses of natural operation and of its acts, or ἐνεργήματα, as all the Fathers, especially St. Maximus and St. John Damascene, testify. We are surprised that Dr. Döllinger was not aware of this when in his pamphlet (pp. 133, 134) he accused Honorius of having twisted the word ἐνέργεια to a different sense.

[26] Die Papst Fabeln des Mittelalters, pp. 132, 133.

one will in Christ." Certainly, it may be undeniable for dreamers who deal with phantoms, mistaking them for living realities, not for such as study historical documents with a mind free from prejudice and a heart free from passion. Our readers shall have the very words of Honorius, and then shall judge for themselves: "Unde et unam voluntatem fatemur Domini nostri Jesu Christi, quia profecto a Divinitate assumpta est nostra natura, non culpa; illa profecto quæ ante peccatum creata est, non quæ post prævaricationem vitiata."[27] Every time we read these words of Honorius, we are amazed that men who profess an extended and scientific knowledge of literature have been able to disguise from themselves the natural and obvious purport of the words. Now it is really undeniable that Pope Honorius does not assert that there is only one will in Christ, and that divine, but on the contrary maintains that in the humanity assumed by the Word there is only one will, and that the spiritual will. His argument is as follows: the Word of God took to Himself our nature, not the sin which is in it; our nature as it was created before sin, not as it was corrupted by transgression. Now, our natural will, the will as a power of our soul, is not a fruit of sin; it was an essential part of human nature, even before this was stained with sin. Hence the Word of God by assuming our nature must have assumed its natural will. Again, the will which is a fruit of sin, and which is called

[27] Epist. Honorii cit. L c. p. 963.

sin in the Scripture, the will which did not exist in human nature in its state of innocence, is our concupiscence. The Word of God, therefore, by assuming our nature could not assume that will; that is to say, our concupiscence.

From this clear and conclusive reasoning it is manifest that Pope Honorius excluded from the Incarnate Word nothing but the will of the flesh, or, in other words, our concupiscences. In fact, he quotes several passages of St. Paul from his Epistle to the Romans (vii. 17 seq.), and the first to the Corinthians (xv. 50), in order to prove that after the first transgression a hard struggle arose in our nature between the fleshly will and that of the mind; these being contrary to each other in their tendencies and desires; whereupon he concludes that in Christ there was no contrariety whatever, since He did not assume the fleshly will. "Non est itaque assumpta, sicut præfati sumus, a Salvatore vitiata natura, quæ repugnaret legi mentis ejus. . . . . Nam lex alia et voluntas diversa non fuit vel contraria Salvatori, quia supra legem natus est humanæ conditionis."[28] Honorius foresaw that an exception could be raised against his assertion founded on the passages of the gospel, "Not as I will, but as Thou wilt;" and "I am not come to do My own will, but the will of Him that sent Me." He answers the objection, by saying that the passages quoted and similar texts do not imply any contrariety of wills in Christ, but that they reveal a peculiar economical design of His assumed

[28] Epist. Honorii, l. c.

humanity (dispensationis, οἰκονομίας, humanitatis assumptæ). "Tota enim," he continues, "propter nos dicta sunt, quibus dedit exemplum, ut sequamur vestigia ejus."[29] The Incarnate Word assumed our humanity, not only that He might be a victim consecrated to His Father's glory, but also in order to become the pattern which we should copy in ourselves. Now Christ became our pattern because He practised what He taught, and by His example He opened the path which we should follow, so that, by perfect submission of His will to the will of His Divine Father, He gave us a great example of perfect resignation to the will of God. But Christ, whilst perfectly complying with His Father's will, had not to endure any struggle with the concupiscence of the flesh, which fights against the wishes of our mind; He did not feel in Himself any such disorderly feeling, even when His will submitted to things which, by themselves, are not agreeable to the original unfallen tendencies of our nature.

The "non quod ego volo" does not imply contrariety of wills in Christ, originating from the law of concupiscence, for this last did not exist in Him; but it only points to what would naturally agree with our inclinations, and please our will. But the very same language (non quod ego volo) transferred to our nature, as it is affected by the Fall, means not merely what in itself is not pleasant to our lawful tendencies, but moreover what is positively and strongly opposed by our fleshly will, which strives to

[29] Epist. Honorii, l. c.

carry with it the will of our mind. What, then, is the meaning Honorius intended in the following passage? "Ista propter nos dicta sunt quibus dedit exemplum ut sequamur vestigia ejus; pius magister discipulos imbuens, ut non suam unusquisque nostrum, sed potius Domini in omnibus præferat voluntatem." First, it cannot mean that there was no human will in Christ; for if Christ had no human will, how could He afford us example of submission to God, and how could we follow His footsteps? But Honorius plainly asserted that we are to do this; therefore he at the same time plainly asserted the existence of a human will in Christ; because where there is no distinction of wills, no submission of any kind can have place. Secondly, according to Honorius, Christ by the above words taught us to contradict our fleshly will, in order to submit our spirit to God. But although Christ could not give us example of the denial of the fleshly will, which He had not, He could give us an instruction and precept; and these He imparted to us in words made stronger by His own example of perfect resignation. His example bears on the submission of the human will to God's will; His instruction points to the battle against our concupiscences, in which we should willingly engage in order to submit our will to God. Such is the true meaning of the doctrine of Honorius, when he acknowledges only one will in Christ's human nature. These are not, as Mr. Renouf says they are, "subterfuges which will not bear examination." The explanation which we have given will defy the examination of a hundred critics like Mr. Renouf, and also of all those who fully understand the real question at issue.

On the following page of Mr. Renouf's pamphlet we find a remark which betrays a strange ignorance of the state of the controversy. "If Honorius," he says, "believed that this was the real question at issue (the existence in Christ of two human and contrary wills), he ought to have condemned Sophronius for manifestly heretical doctrine."[80] Mr. Renouf is quite wrong in attributing to those who have given the foregoing explanation of the passage in question the belief that Honorius ever thought that to be the question at issue. What the Pope says against the existence of two contrary wills in Christ's human nature has nothing to do with the Monothelite controversy. But Honorius having spoken, according to St. Leo's doctrine, of the unity of person in Christ, and of the diversity of His natures hypostatically united, was brought by his subject to speak of the integrity of His assumed nature.

Some writers have made it their business to blacken the memory of Pope Honorius, and have followed the Monothelite Pyrrhus in distorting the meaning of the words we have cited—"unam voluntatem fatemur Domini nostri Jesu Christi"—in order to fasten upon them a Monothelite meaning. Honorius is in no way accountable for this : his meaning was quite different. If Mr. Renouf will deign to listen to our advice, he will put aside all precon-

[80] The Condemnation of Pope Honorius, p. 16.

ceived views, and read carefully the letters of Pope Honorius: he will soon be convinced that what he has represented as *undeniable* is false; what he has called *absurd* is right; what he has qualified as *untruth* is the truth; and what he has declared to be Monothelism is the Catholic doctrine. But in historical controversies, when it happens that the perversity of man has misrepresented facts, the testimony of contemporaries is the most satisfactory means of arriving at the truth; and when the clear language of documents concurs with the evidence of contemporaries, no doubt can remain; in such case the narrative cannot properly be said to establish the truth of what we read in the documents, but only to ratify and confirm it. We have an instance of this in the controverted passage of Pope Honorius on one will in Christ. The passage itself tells its own meaning, as we have seen, independently of any external evidence. The testimony, therefore, of contemporary authorities must have still greater power to put the truth of the explanation beyond all doubt. With this view we can refer to the evidence of St. Maximus, who after the death of Sophronius was the great doctor of the Eastern Church, the leader of the Catholics against the Monothelite faction, the man who, after having convinced Pyrrhus, the Monothelite Patriarch of Constantinople, that he had been upholding error, persuaded him to place a written retractation in the hands of Pope Theodore,[31]

[31] Conc. Lat. Secr. i. (Labbo, t. vii. p. 91.) Hist. Miscell. Pauli Diaconi, l. xviii. ed. Migne, in t. xcv. PP. LL. p. 1042. Anast.

the man who suffered persecution and finally martyrdom for the faith.[82] In like manner we can refer to the testimony of Pope John IV., who succeeded Honorius in the pontifical See after the two-months' reign of Severinus, and who wrote and addressed to the Emperor Constantine an apology in favour of Honorius against the calumnious letter of Patriarch Pyrrhus. Finally, we can bring forward the evidence of Abbot John, secretary both to Honorius and to John IV., who drew up the letter addressed by Honorius to Sergius, and who could not fail to understand its purport correctly, while his character affords us a guarantee of his veracity; for, as we learn from St. Maximus, he was a man who had illustrated all the West with his virtues and religious doctrine.[83] Now St. Maximus, Pope John IV., and Abbot John, all testify most clearly that Pope Honorius, when asserting one will in Christ our Lord, had in view the sacred humanity only, in which he denied the existence of two contrary wills.[84] What contemporary witnesses could be found whose evidence upon this

Bibl. in Vita Theodori Papæ, ed. Migne, in t. cxxviii. PP. LL. p. 723.

[82] See Vita et Certamen S. Maximi et Acta ejusdem (in Op. S. Maximi, t. i. ed. Migne, t. xc. PP. LL. p. 68 sqq.).

[83] μετὰ τῶν ἄλλων αὐτῶν καλῶν, καὶ τοῖς τῆς εὐσεβείας δόγμασι πᾶσαν τὴν δύσιν καταφαιδρύνων. Disputatio cum Pyrrho (Op. t. ii. l. c. p. 329). Tomus dogmaticus ad Marinum Presbyt. (Op. t. ii. ed. Migne, l. c. p. 244.)

[84] S. Maximus, Tomus cit. ad Marinum, p. 237. Disput. cum Pyrrho, l. c. p. 328. Joannis IV. Apologia pro Honorio Papa ad Constantinum. (Labbe, t. vi. p. 1511 sq.) Abbatis Joannis verba in Disp. cum Pyrrho, l. c.

subject ought to have more weight in the balance of history and good sense? The learned Garnier had good reason not to hesitate to call them *tres locupletissimos testes* in favour of the orthodoxy of Pope Honorius.[85] But in the pages of Mr. Renouf's pamphlet we have prejudice instead of history, passion in the place of good sense; hence it is that this writer sets no value on the evidence of these three witnesses. " The evidence," he says, " of the *tres locupletissimi testes* is really that of one man, and that one an interested and mendacious witness. St. Maximus, when confronted with the authority of Pope Honorius, appeals to the evidence of Abbot John as having really written the letter of Honorius to Sergius, and therefore being the best judge of its meaning. This very man was also secretary to Pope John IV., and wrote a letter in this Pope's name, giving a lying account of the controversy, and explaining away the letter of Honorius."[86] This passage is one tissue of impudent assertion, suppression of truth, and blundering error. It is sheer impudence to apply the terms "interested and mendacious witness" and "liar"[87] to the Abbot John, a man who in his own age was held in such high esteem both in West and East; it is a piece of insolence to give the lie to the learned martyr St. Maximus, who thought so highly of the character of the

[85] Garnier S.J. Dissertatio ii. ad Librum Diurnum, n. xxxii. ed. Migne cit. p. 153.
[86] The Condemnation of Pope Honorius, pp. 15, 16.
[87] In his letter to the *Westminster Gazette*, dated June 20th, Mr. Renouf again called Abbot John an interested liar.

Abbot John as to call him a most holy man (ἁγιώτατον).

Mr. Renouf is further guilty of suppressing the truth. He has, he tells us, "thoroughly mastered the literature of the subject," and must therefore have read the letter of St. Maximus to the priest Marinus. Well, in that letter the learned martyr, "confronted with the authority of Pope Honorius, does not merely appeal to the evidence of Abbot John," but fully examines the passage in question. He shows, from the very expressions of Pope Honorius and the context of his letter, that no Monothelite sense can be given to the doctrine there expressed; that Honorius evidently speaks of one will in Christ's humanity; and he quotes a passage from St. Anastasius, who used the like language when writing against Apollinaris.[58] Then, after having discussed the true Catholic meaning of Honorius' letter through more than four pages, he refers to the authority of Abbot Anastasius and Abbot John, not in order to prove his thesis, but in order to confirm it and put it more beyond dispute.[60] In proof of this we remark that St. Maximus, before adducing those witnesses, openly declared himself fully persuaded that what he gave was the true sense of the passage of Honorius, and he does not entertain the

[58] μονονουχὶ συμφθεγγόμενος τῷ μεγάλῳ Ἀθανασίῳ γράφοντι τάδι κατ' Ἀπολιναρίου τοῦ δυσσεβοῦς, &c. Tomus cit. ad Marinum, l. c. p. 240.

[60] βεβαιότερον δέ μοι τοῦτον (νοῦν) πεποίηκεν. . . . Ἀναστάσιος, &c. l. c. p. 244.

least suspicion to the contrary.[40] Why did Mr. Renouf suppress this evidence of the holy martyr, and mention only the passage taken from his dispute with Pyrrhus? In that dispute the learned doctor was satisfied with opposing the authority of the holy and learned John, who had written the letter of Honorius, to the interpretation of Pyrrhus and other Byzantine writers who had given it a wrong meaning. That was at the time sufficient for the purpose of St. Maximus, who intended to confute with the authority of a holy and learned man, the actual writer of the letter of Honorius, the Byzantine Monothelites, who had put a fanciful interpretation, in accordance with their wishes, upon the words of Honorius. And he attained his end, since Pyrrhus, moved by the weight of such a witness, confessed the mistake of his predecessor and surrendered. It seems as if Mr. Renouf was purposely endeavouring to conceal this result. In the letter, however, addressed to Marinus, St. Maximus explained the whole question at length. But Mr. Renouf, with a somewhat lax notion of literary honesty, has kept the evidence hidden from the eyes of his readers. Finally, is it true that Pope John or his secretary gave a lying account of the controversy? It is evidently false. The *Apologia pro Honorio Papa*, written in the name of John IV., may be divided into two parts: the first points out the meaning of the passage of the letter of Honorius

[40] καὶ οὕτω μὲν ἔγωγε τὸν νοῦν ἔχειν ὑπολαμβάνω, πάσης ὄντα καθαρὸν ὑποψίας. l. c.

which had been misrepresented by Pyrrhus; the latter demonstrates the opposition which exists between the doctrine of Honorius and the error of the Monothelites, which is shown to be a disguised Eutychianism and Severianism.

It is in this second portion that the writer states the true view of the controversy: "Quia enim unam voluntatem dicunt divinitatis Christi et humanitatis, et unam simul operationem, quid aliud nisi quia et unam naturam Christi Dei secundum Eutychianam et Severianam divisionem operari noscuntur?"[41] This Apology of Pope John IV., as we said above, was written when Pyrrhus published an extract from the letter of Honorius to Sergius, with the purpose of showing that the Pope had taught only one will in Christ. The apologist therefore was bound to prove, first, that Honorius had not asserted the unity of the will in the divinity and humanity of Christ, but in the humanity alone, which the Word assumed totally free from concupiscence; secondly, that this doctrine had nothing to do with the error of the Monothelites, who denied any will and active operation in the humanity of Christ, and necessarily admitted the errors of Severus.

In the two parts of the Apology he handled successively these two points; and it cannot be said that in so doing he gave a lying account of the controversy. Mr. Renouf has fallen into a gross and unjustifiable mistake. Moreover, how can it be said

---

[41] Apologia pro Honorio Papa. (Labbe, t. vi. p. 1514.)

that the evidence of St. Maximus, of Pope John IV., and of Abbot John, is really that of one man? It cannot be maintained that either the Saint or the Pope wrote in the name of the Abbot John, nor that they threw upon him the responsibility of their assertions. Each of them pledged his own credit in the defence of Pope Honorius which they put forward. Their language is absolute and without reserve, as became men who were thoroughly familiar with the whole controversy. It is absurd, therefore, to assert that "their evidence is really that of one man." But we must not feel surprise at the dogmatic manner in which Mr. Renouf disposes of the external evidence in favour of the orthodoxy of Pope Honorius; he has asserted or suppressed exactly what Dr. Döllinger in his well-known pamphlet *Die Papst Fabeln* had already asserted or suppressed. It is not so much the English School-Inspector as the Munich Professor that treats with so much contempt the evidence of St. Maximus no less than that of Pope John and of the Abbot John; that stigmatises the latter as a liar; that regards as absurd the explanation given by Pope John of the doctrine of Honorius; that suppresses what St. Maximus wrote of Honorius in his dogmatic treatise addressed to Marinus, as well as the conversion of Pyrrhus and his retractation, caused by the authoritative evidence of Abbot John, quoted by the saintly martyr; and that speaks of the triple evidence we have adduced as being that of one man.[42] Mr.

[42] Döllinger, Die Papst Fabeln, p. 134.

Renouf indeed tells us that he had not seen the *Papst Fabeln* before he wrote his *Condemnation of Pope Honorius;* we must therefore conclude that some great similarity of character exists between the two writers which has led to their independent adoption of the same line of argument, which derives what force it has wholly from the same baseless assertions and unwarrantable suppressions.

Mr. Renouf was not content with finding Monothelite tenets in the vexed passage of the letter of Honorius, and with casting contempt on all those who maintained its orthodox interpretation, but he also thought he saw in the confession of Honorius an identity of idea with the *Ecthesis* and the *Typus;* and he went so far as to assert that "one of the most important parts of the Ecthesis is copied *verbatim* from the letter of Honorius."[43] His friend Dr. Döllinger had said before him that the doctrine of Honorius had given origin to the two imperial decrees called the Ecthesis of Heraclius and the Typus of Constans,[44] because, as he imagined, the letter of Honorius gave the Emperor ground to believe that the Roman See would not oppose the doctrinal rule of the Ecthesis. This is the whole foundation for what Mr. Renouf asserts as to the identity of doctrine of the letter of Honorius and of the two imperial edicts. But it is a mere

[43] The Condemnation of Pope Honorius, pp. 14, 15, 23 note.
[44] "Diese dem Sergius und den übrigen Gönnern und Anhängern des Monotheletismus willkommene Lehre des Honorius führte zu den beiden kaiserlichen Edikten, der Ekthesis und dem Typus." l. c. p. 133.

calumny, which can be quickly dispelled by simply confronting the Pope's letter with the imperial decrees. The Ecthesis of Heraclius, it cannot be denied, contains no more error than what is insinuated in the letter of Sergius to Pope Honorius, and other missives of the same prelate; but it is in perfect contradiction to the doctrine expressed by Honorius in his letters to Sergius. This Pope, as we have proved above, clearly taught a twofold operation in Christ, one belonging to the divinity, and the other to the humanity; although the Person of Christ being one, the Operator is one. If he speaks of one will in Christ, he refers to the humanity, where there cannot be two contrary wills in a state of struggle and reluctance. The Ecthesis, on the other hand, maintains a doctrine altogether opposite. It states that all the operation of Christ, divine and human, must be attributed to the Word Incarnate alone, and therefore it did not permit any other profession of faith. Moreover it declares, in conformity with that erroneous and heretical tenet, that, if we confess two operations in Christ, we must necessarily admit in His Person two contrary wills; and hence it openly maintains one will only in Christ.[45]

We are not anxious to enlarge on this exposition by pointing out the contradictions to be found in the

[45] Ecthesis Heraclii, in Conc. Lat. Secr. iii. (Labbe, t. vii. p. 204.) 'Ἀλλὰ γὰρ καὶ ἐπειδὴ ταύτῃ τὸ καὶ δύο ἐριζόντων διλήματα ἐκεντίως πρὸς ἄλληλα ἔχοντων. . . . καὶ ἐντεῦθεν δύο τοῦ τἀναντία θέλοντος εἰσάγεσθαι, ὅπερ δυσσεβὲς ὑπάρχει καὶ ἀλλότριον τοῦ χριστιανικοῦ δόγματος; . . . ὅθεν . . . ἓν θέλημα τοῦ Κυρίου ἡμῶν Ἰησοῦ Χριστοῦ τοῦ ἀληθινοῦ Θεοῦ ὁμολογοῦμεν. l. c. p. 205.

Ecthesis, a document in which the Patriarch Sergius, its author, summed up his errors and made them a law of the State. All who read this section will readily acknowledge that we find in that iniquitous document the mind of Sergius rather than that of Honorius. Mr. Renouf, however, is under an obligation of proving that the most important passages of the Ecthesis are taken verbatim from the letter of Honorius.

Let us pass on to consider the case of the Typus of Constans. Mr. Renouf assures us that the position taken up in this document is exactly that of Pope Honorius, whose authority, he says, it followed. This time Mr. Renouf chances to be more moderate in his language than Dr. Döllinger, who has charged Honorius with having gone far beyond the limits of the Typus.[46] Nevertheless, both Mr. Renouf and Dr. Döllinger agree in this, that Honorius as well as the Typus prohibit the discussion of one or two wills and operations. We, however, maintain, on the other side, that their difference concerns what is substantial and peculiar to each of them.

The Typus was the work of the Monothelite Patriarch Paul, successor of Pyrrhus, but it was published in the name of the Emperor Constans. This prince, with the purpose of furthering his political views, usurped a right which belongs to the supreme ecclesiastical authority alone—a right to which the civil powers are bound to yield respect, and cannot control by the power of the sword. Constans, by en-

[46] Die Papst Fabeln, p. 136.

forcing the Typus, and substituting it for the Ecthesis, made himself a most powerful instrument of the Monothelite faction. The Typus, indeed, has an appearance of placing the doctrinal element more in the background, and of aiming only at putting an end to violent disputes, and restoring peace to the Church. It does not appear to favour either Monothelism or Dithelism; it decides in favour of neither, but strictly and under the most heavy penalties forbids the holding and defending of either of the two contrary views of the controversy, and prohibits all further contention on these points.[47] We need say nothing here of the injustice and tyranny of the prince who signed and sanctioned that decree. We will consider the Typus in its doctrinal purport only, and with reference to the Monothelite dogmas. The Typus contains the words "operation" and "will" (ἐνέργεια, θέλημα), in the sense of the physical, internal power of nature, and natural active faculty. Therefore, by forbidding the profession of two operations and wills in Christ, it not only places a Catholic doctrine on the same level with the heresy which admits one single operation and will in Christ, but it also forbids the subjects of the Empire to profess in our Lord what is essential to the existence of His two natures; and consequently it forbids the profession of the faith of Chalcedon and of the dogmatical letter of Pope Leo, in which that essential doctrine is expressly stated. 'The Typus, then, be-

[47] See the Typus, in Conc. Lat. Secr. iv. (Labbe, t. vii. p. 237 seq.)

sides the unchristian indifferentism, which was the root from which it sprang, embodied a skilful artifice to check for the time being the assertion of the Catholic truth, in order to open the way to heresy; and this after the solemn condemnation pronounced by the Popes Severinus and John IV. against the errors of the Monothelites. The character, therefore, of the Typus was manifestly heretical, and it deserved to be stigmatised as blasphemous and most impious by the Lateran Council under Martin I.

Now we would ask Mr. Renouf and Dr. Döllinger to point out to us the place in which Pope Honorius forbade the profession of two wills in Christ. We would remind both of what we have said in the beginning of this section, namely, that Honorius not only never forbade the profession of two operations in Christ our Lord, but also declared it to be a duty of every Catholic to believe and confess them, according to St. Leo's doctrine. We would inform them that when Honorius suggests the expediency of refraining from the expression, "one or two operations," he did not employ the word "operation," or ἐνέργεια, in the sense of the internal power of a nature, but in the sense of its external acts; which, if referred to the person, may be summed up into one operation, as the operator is one; but if referred to the two natures, may be said to be two or more operations, according to the multiple mode of working of the two natures. Hence he says it is useless to inquire whether, on account of the working of Christ's divinity and humanity, there should be said to be one or

Honorius' two Letters to Sergius. 71

two derived operations; for this reason he adds that there is no canon of a Council in the matter, and that the Scripture teaches the contrary; and this is why he asserts that the expression, "one or two operations," is a novelty which may turn out dangerous to the faith.[48]

In the whole of this passage, as we have proved above, the Pope does not allude to the physical internal operations of Christ, but to the external acts. Dr. Döllinger, we have already said, himself acknowledged what we here state; and it is somewhat remarkable that his admiring disciple Mr. Renouf has not profited by his master's lesson, and so escaped falling into a lower depth of blunder than the author of the *Papst Fabeln* has reached.

Let us conclude. The Typus prohibits the confession of two operations in Christ; Honorius commands that they should be confessed and preached. The Typus speaks of operations (ἐνεργειῶν) in the sense of substantial virtue of nature (οὐσιώδης ἐνέργεια); Honorius speaks of them in the sense of acts, and distinguishes between the operation peculiar to each nature. The Typus prohibits the confession of a doctrine of faith with reference both to the two natural operations and to the two wills of Christ; Honorius merely advises abstinence from forms of expression which do not belong to the ecclesiastical dogma. Does all this show an identity of tenet, and not rather an essential opposition?

From what we have said of the orthodoxy of

---

[48] Epist. i. Honorii, in Conc. vi. act. xii. (Labbo, t. vii. p. 063.)

Pope Honorius, our readers may conclude that the position of our adversaries is quite untenable; and that there exists such an accumulation of various evidence in favour of the Pontiff, that the maintenance of the opposite view implies a large amount of obstinate prejudice. We shall, however, be repaid if we institute a still further inquiry as to the opinions held by the contemporaries of Honorius regarding the faith of the Pope. And first let us consider what was the judgment of Sergius, the Patriarch of Constantinople. It is undeniable that this prelate was convinced of the thorough orthodoxy of Honorius, and of his being in no way inclined to the Monothelite views. Had not this been so, Sergius would have made a point of circulating the letters of Honorius throughout the East, whereas he withdrew them as much as possible from the knowledge of the public. If it be true that the doctrine held by Honorius is really identical with that of the Ecthesis, why did not the writer of that document claim the support of the papal authority, or why was its publication delayed until after the death of the very Pope who is said to have been its patron?[49] But we need not confine ourselves to negative arguments, for the records of the time afford us more positive testimonies. Sophronius, Patriarch of Jerusalem, and the great leader of the Catholics in the struggle against the Monothelite error, must have been ac-

---

[49] Honorius I. died in 638; the Ecthesis was published in 639, nearly as soon as the Pope's death was known in Constantinople.

quainted with the letters and teaching of Pope Honorius. Yet Sophronius, as we have seen, sent Stephen, Bishop of Dora, to Honorius, to urge upon the Pope the necessity of passing a definitive sentence on the disputed points. We have quoted above the terms in which he spoke of the Roman See, "where the foundations are laid of the orthodox faith." Now if Sophronius entertained the least suspicion that Pope Honorius was himself infected with the error, he would certainly not have sent to him a solemn embassy in order to obtain his definitive judgment in a matter of faith. Nor must it be thought that any different opinion was held by St. Maximus, the successor of Sophronius in the defence of the Catholic cause, and heir alike of his doctrine and his zeal.

The Patriarch Pyrrhus had already spread abroad a most grievous calumny against the memory of Honorius. Extracts from his letters were being circulated both in the East and in the West, and were exciting suspicions against the faith of that Pope; hence Maximus, as the leader of the Catholics against the Monothelite faction, was bound to make public the common persuasion with regard to the doctrine and orthodoxy of Honorius. Now St. Maximus declared himself the apologist of the Pope whose orthodoxy he defended in his dispute with Pyrrhus; he returned to the subject in his dogmatic *Tomus* to the Priest Marinus; he insisted on the same point in the Epistle "ad Petrum illustrem." In this letter he represented Pope Honorius as not only unstained with any blemish of Monothelism, but also as one of the zealous Pontiffs who resisted that heresy, and endeavoured to bring its author into the path of truth.[50] After proof of this, the assertion of Dr. Döllinger must seem strange indeed when he says that, whilst all the West, and principally Rome, arose vigorously to oppose and condemn Monothelism, Pope Honorius alone showed favour to it, and was on this account abandoned by all.[51] But if so, how is it that the Romans, after his death, compared him with St. Gregory the Great for his doctrine as well as for his virtues; and expressed sentiments of praise and admiration for him in an epigraph engraven on his sepulchre?[52] Had they entertained the least doubt of his orthodoxy, nothing

[50] "Quæ hos non rogavit Ecclesia? quis pius et orthodoxus non supplicavit antistes, cessare illos a propria hæresi clamando et obtestando? Quid autem et divinus Honorius, quid vero post illum Severinus senex, quid denique et is qui post hunc extitit sacer Joannes?"—Ex Epist. ad Petrum illustrem. (Op. t. ii. ed. Migne, L. c. p. 143.)

[51] Die Papst Fabeln, p. 134.

[52] "Pastorem magnum laudis pia præmia lustrant,
    Cui functus Petri hac vice summa tenet;
Effulget tumulis nam præsul Honorius istis,
    Cujus magnanimum nomen honorque manet.
Sedis Apostolicæ meritis nam jura gubernans,
    Dispersos revocat, optima lucra refert,
Utque sagax animo divino in carmine pollens,
    Ad vitam pastor ducere novit oves.
Histria nam dudum sacro sub schismate fossa,
    Ad statuta patrum teque monente redit . . .
Quem doctrina potens, quem sacræ regula vitæ
    Pontificum pariter sanxit habere decus,
Sanctiloqui semper in te commenta magistri
    Emicuere tui tamque fecunda nimis.
Nam Gregorii tanti vestigia justi
    Dum sequeris cupiens et meritumque geris," &c.

of the kind would have been written on his tomb, nor would the Romans have immortalised with lying praise the name of a heretic. Lastly, the successors of Honorius in the chair of St. Peter lent their authority to confirm the high character for orthodoxy and virtue which the public voice gave to Honorius. Thus Pope John IV. testifies to the scandal given to all Christendom when the heretical leader Pyrrhus dared to appeal to Honorius as a supporter of his errors.[53] Pope Martin opening the Lateran Council, did not hesitate to assert that his predecessors had most constantly resisted the Monothelite errors, and had endeavoured to bring their authors into the path of truth.[54] To speak thus of his predecessors without exception or limitation would have been impossible, had he believed that Honorius betrayed the Catholic truth; especially seeing that Pyrrhus had already charged Honorius with Monothelism, and that his successor Paul, in his letter to Pope Theodore, had appealed to Honorius as a witness in favour of the same heresy.[55] Under these circumstances the declaration of Pope Martin was designed to dissipate

[53] Apologia pro Honorio. (Labbe, t. vi. p. 1514.)
[54] In Conc. Lat. Secr. i. (Labbe, t. vii. p. 94.) "Ideoque in scripto vel sine scripto orthodoxorum preces minime despicientes Apostolicæ memoriæ nostri decessores non destiterunt prædictis viris diversis temporibus consultissime scribentes et tam rogantes, quamque regulariter increpantes, necnon per apocrisiarios suos, ut dictum est, per hoc maxime destinatos præsentialiter admonentes et contestantes quatenus proprium emendarent novitatis commentum, atque catholicam fidem catholicæ ecclesiæ remearent."
[55] Epist. Patr. Pauli ad Theodorum, in Conc. Lat. Secr. iv. (Labbe, l. c. p. 233.)

all doubt regarding the orthodoxy of Honorius. His general assertion, considering the time in which it was made, is equivalent to what St. Maximus advanced in favour of Honorius in his Epistle "ad Petrum illustrem." Pope Agatho also shows himself equally convinced of the orthodoxy of Honorius. In his dogmatic letter addressed to the Emperor Pogonatus, which was read in the Sixth Synod, he testified to the solicitude of all his predecessors in repressing the new heresy, and he mentions especially their suggesting silence to the partisans of error.[56] By these words he undoubtedly referred to Honorius; and although he did not say whether the economy adopted by Honorius had been well-advised and calculated to attain its end, yet it is undeniable that he gave the most favourable evidence of the orthodoxy of that Pope. Had he felt any misgivings on that score, he could not have classed Honorius with John IV., Theodore, and Martin I., as one of those who opposed Monothelism; he could not have said that Honorius by his policy of silence intended to check the Monothelite heresy, had he thought him a Monothelite. So then, the orthodoxy of Pope Honorius was publicly and repeatedly testified to by all his contemporaries till the very opening of the Sixth Council. Throughout that interval no

---

[56] "Undo et Apostolicæ memoriæ meæ parvitatis prædecessores, dominicis doctrinis instructi . . . . . . nunquam neglexerunt eos (Monothelitas) hortari atque obsecrando commonere, ut a pravi dogmatis hæretico errore, *saltem tacendo desisterent*." Epist. Agathonis Papæ ad Constantinum, in act. iv. conc. vi. (Labbe, t. vii. p. 603.)

one Catholic called it in question, while it was expressly defended against the attacks of Pyrrhus and Paul by the principal leaders and martyrs of the orthodox party, and the Popes, who were most energetic in their opposition to the heresy.

We must here notice a difficulty raised by Mr. Renouf. " The fact," he says, " that Pope Martin I. and the Lateran Council heard Honorius quoted in a 'dogmatic letter' as an authority for Monothelism without any contradiction being offered, is a sure sign that his cause was no longer held to be defensible."[57] The same remark had been made also by Dr. Döllinger, who seems desirous of suggesting some charge of injustice against the Lateran Council.[58] We must, however, confess that Dr. Döllinger in his way of putting the point was somewhat more honest than Mr. Renouf. First, this last-named writer mentions a "dogmatic letter," in which Honorius is quoted as an authority for Monothelism. Allusion is here made to the letter of the Patriarch Paul, the author of the Typus; but we do not know any ground for asserting that this letter was ever called "dogmatic" by the Lateran Council. Certainly the Bishops who required it to be read called it simply "letter" (ἐπιστολήν). Pope Martin ordered to be read "the letter of Paul" (epistolam Pauli). Theophylact, the prothonotary of the Apostolic See, declared that he had in his hands the "letter of Paul." The letter itself bears no other title than "letter of Paul of Constantinople to

---

[57] The Condemnation of Pope Honorius, p. 17.
[58] Die Papst Fabeln, pp. 134-136.

Pope Theodore."[59] The Bishop Deusdedit, speaking of the document, called it a "letter."[60] The epithet "dogmatic" does not appear anywhere. Again, Mr. Renouf does not tell us that the "dogmatic" letter in which Honorius is quoted as an authority for Monothelism, is the letter of a Monothelite Bishop, the author of the Typus, who, like Pyrrhus, calumniated that Pope. Thirdly, he does not notice (nor does Dr. Döllinger) that in the letter quoted the Patriarch Paul not only appeals to Honorius but also to St. Gregory Nazianzen, to St. Athanasius, to St. Cyril of Alexandria, and in short to all the Fathers and Doctors of the Church, as partisans of the Monothelite view.[61] Now we may retort the argument against Mr. Renouf in this manner. The Fathers of the Lateran Council heard without any contradiction the names of St. Gregory, St. Cyril, St. Athanasius, and the rest, quoted as authorities for Monothelism, and yet no one believes this to be a sure sign that the cause of these holy Doctors was no longer held to be defensible: in the same manner then in the case of Honorius. This is not all: there is another argument which may help to show the rashness of the inference so confidently drawn by Dr. Döllinger, and adopted with equal confidence by his pupil. Pope Martin beyond doubt well knew what the Byzantine Patriarch Paul had written against Honorius in his letter to Pope Theodore, and on this account, as we said above,

[59] Conc. Lat. Secr. iv. p. 227 seq.
[60] Ib. p. 235.
[61] In Conc. Lat. Secr. iv. (Labbe, vii. p. 233.)

after the opening of the Council, he made a solemn declaration in favour of *all* his predecessors, in order to reject beforehand the infamous charge of the Monothelite champion. Moreover, the Pope with all the Synod condemned Paul and his letter, but no one thought it necessary to mention the name of Honorius. This argument will gain still more strength if we remark that Pope Martin, after the opening of the Synod, explicitly declared that it was his intention and that of the whole Council to discover and bring to light all the authors of the Monothelite heresy.[62] He mentions the four Patriarchs, Sergius, Cyrus, Pyrrhus, and Paul, but he does not use a word directed against Honorius. In the course of the Council itself many *Libelli* were read, all concerning the Monothelite controversy. We may consult those of Stephen of Dora from Palestine;[63] of the Monks and Abbots of Africa, of Palestine and Armenia;[64] of Victor Bishop of Carthage;[65] of Sergius of Cyprus;[66] of Maurus of Ravenna;[67] the Synodical Letters of the Councils of Numidia, of Mauritania, and of Byzacene.[68] In all these Libelli and Synodical Letters the Roman See is spoken of as the foundation of faith, as the teacher of truth, as the centre of Catholic doctrine;[69] in all of them the four Patriarchs are

---

[62] Conc. Lat. Secr. i. (Labbe, l. c. p. 86.) "Oportet eos in aperto fieri manifestos."
[63] Conc. Lat. Secr. ii. (Labbe, l. c. p. 106.)
[64] Ib. (Labbe, l. c. p. 117.)   [65] Ib. p. 155 seq.
[66] Ib. p. 125 seq.   [67] Ib. p. 130 seq.   [68] Ib. pp. 131, 142.
[69] Ib. pp. 108, 118, 159, &c.

unanimously denounced, together with other partisans and promoters of the new heresy. But we find no allusion, direct or indirect, to Pope Honorius. This omission cannot be explained except by supposing that no one considered the doctrine of Honorius deserving of such denunciation. We must not, then, follow Mr. Renouf in believing that at the time of the Lateran Council the cause of Honorius was held to be no longer defensible; on the contrary, it was then considered that no plausible ground could be found for any charge of heresy against him.

IV.

The Sixth Synod and the Condemnation of Pope Honorius.

The Eastern Church had been kept continually in a state of terrible confusion for about sixty years by the Monothelite faction (622-680); and the imperial power, which had been led by considerations of worldly interest to abet the heresy, had reaped the natural fruit of its rebellion against the Church in domestic strife and interior weakness. The Ecthesis of the Patriarch Sergius, published by the Emperor Heraclius, had increased the general confusion; and the Typus of the Patriarch Paul, to which the Emperor Constans gave the force of an imperial law, had failed to restore calm and concord in the provinces of the East: both these documents, the Ecthesis and the Typus, by favouring Monothelism, had rendered the state of affairs more desperate than ever, and spread still further the internal cancer which had for so long a time been corroding the vital organs of the Byzantine Empire. In fact, whilst the Emperors and their Patriarchs were attacking Catholic doctrine and abetting schism, the Greek provinces were being torn from the unity of the Empire; and now the Emperors, who had put forth all their zeal against the supporters of the Catholic dogma, proved powerless to resist the enemies of their people. The Popes on their side had spared no means in order to recall the erring factions back to the path of faith and unity. They had repeatedly condemned the Ecthesis and the Typus, as well as the authors of the Monothelite heresies. After many provincial Synods had been fruitlessly held at Rome against the new error, Martin I. summoned a Universal Council in the Lateran Palace (654), where, at the head of 105 Bishops, he anathematised the errors of Monothelism with their authors, and formally defined the doctrine delivered by Catholic tradition as a rule of faith, thus binding the conscience of the whole Christian world. The authority attributed in the Church to this Synod was so great, that it was inserted after the four previous General Councils in the Pontifical Profession of Faith.[1] But its dogmatic decrees were far from being received by the Emperor Constans with faith and

[1] Liber Diurnus Romani PP. c. ii. tit. 9, in iii. Prof. fidei. (Migne, PP. LL. t. cv. p. 58.)

obedience; on the contrary, they increased his hostility to the Catholic doctrine, and gave rise to a confusion greater than any previous. The records of history tell us of the sufferings of the illustrious Pontiff Martin; of the great champion of the faith Maximus, with his two disciples both named Athanasius; and of the other glorious martyrs who at that time received their crowns at the hands of the imperial heretic. The blood of those heroic confessors secured the rapid triumph of the faith. Shortly after their glorious martyrdom Constans received the recompense of his crimes in a miserable death,[2] and the state of the Eastern Church underwent a complete change. Constantine Pogonatus, a prince nurtured in Catholic principles, took the helm of the Empire, and without delay applied to the See of Rome for the restoration of Catholic union in the Oriental Church. He addressed a letter to Pope Donus, requesting him to send legates to Constantinople, in order to put an end to the Monothelite controversy and restore peace to the Empire. But when the imperial letters arrived at Rome, Pope Agatho had already succeeded Donus. Agatho received the proposal of the Emperor with favour, and accordingly in 680 he assembled a Council of 125 Bishops at Rome, with the purpose of choosing his legates and of settling the points of faith to be solemnly decreed in the Œcumenical Synod. Then by the authority of the Pope the Sixth General Council was opened at

[2] Codrenus, Hist. Comp. t. i. p. 763. ed. Bonn. Hist. Miscella. l. xix. p. 1052. (PP. LL. Migne, t. xcv.)

Constantinople on the 7th day of November in the year 680. The Emperor Constantine in this Synod held the presidency of honour, and sat in the centre of the assembly, as the great Constantine had done at Nicæa. But it would be most wrong to think that he held the presidency of jurisdiction and by right. We should be surprised to hear Mr. Renouf avow such an opinion; but if he does not hold it, we do not understand why he is so anxious to inform us that "the Emperor presided in all the Sessions at which he was present;" and "that he had his way in all things when present;" that during his absence he was represented by two patricians and two ex-consuls, and that "Bishops were very small persons indeed."[3] And again, that "the legates of the Pope and of the See of Jerusalem sat on the left of the Emperor, the Patriarchs of Constantinople and Antioch, &c. on the right."[4]

We are thankful to Mr. Renouf for this valuable information, for which he has kindly found room in his notable twenty-six pages against Pope Honorius. But if he thinks that the Legates of the Pope did not really preside in the Council, because they sat on the left of the Emperor, he is grossly deceived. This false impression will be at once dispelled if we merely look at the list of the signatures of the members of the Council appended to the definition of faith and to the Prosphonetic Letter sent to the Emperor. In both these documents the names of the Pontifical Legates are the first in the list, preceding even the

[3] The Condemnation of Pope Honorius, pp. 2, 10.   [4] l. c. p. 2.

names of all the Eastern Patriarchs. On the other hand, the name of the Emperor is written in the formula of faith below those of all the Bishops; and by his signature he only expresses his consent to the decree, without the least show of authority in sanctioning a definition of faith.[5] But the Bishops declare that they sign the formula of faith *defining* it; and the Legates signed in the name of Pope Agatho, whose authority they represented.[6] Therefore the presidency of the Emperor was merely honorary, without any indication of power or jurisdiction. Constantine Pogonatus could not forget the traditions of the Empire. His predecessors had openly declared, that if they attended the general assembly of the Bishops, they did it, not in order to display any authority of their own in ecclesiastical matters, but with the purpose of shielding the authority of the Fathers with that of the Empire.[7] If he, like his predecessors, misled by the example of Constantine I., thought it his right to occupy the first place in the general synods, neither he nor they harboured the idea of having jurisdiction over them as presidents. It is true that the writer of the history of the Sixth Synod, by the expression προκαθημένου Κωνσταντίνου may seem to mean "under the presidency of Con-

---

[5] Conc. Constant. iii. act. xviii. (Labbe, t. vii. pp. 1063 seq., 1094 seq.) ἀνέγνωμεν καὶ συνῃνέσαμεν (p. 1080).

[6] ὁρίσας ὑπέγραψα... τὸν τόπον ἐπέχων Ἀγάθωνος... ὑπέγραψα.

[7] See in especial manner Allocutio Marciani Imp. in act. iv. Conc. Chalced. (Labbe, t. iv. p. 1476.) His words are quoted by Gratian in his Decretum, p. i. dist. xcvi. can. ii.

stantine;"[8] but προκαθίζειν does not mean properly "to preside," but simply "to sit down before," or "in front."—"to sit in public." In fact, in the twelfth, thirteenth, and fourteenth sessions of the same Council, when the Emperor was absent, the same word is referred to his seat;[9] and of course the seat does not preside, though it was placed in an honourable position. Therefore in the fifteenth session the writer, when speaking of the imperial seat during the absence of Constantine, uses the word προτεθειμένου.[10]

But it is idle to insist further upon a subject which we believe we have already made clear enough. With regard to the left side of the Emperor being appointed for the Papal Legates, Mr. Renouf is, as usual, at fault: it is well known that in those times the left side was regarded as the more honourable. According to the ancient *Ordo Romanus*, in public ecclesiastical assemblies the Bishops were to sit on the left, and the priests on the right.[11]

A more important question now demands an answer, the solution of which will cast great light on the subject in hand. Pope Agatho, after the council held at Rome, sent his Legates to the Œcumenical Synod assembled in Constantinople. What character were these Legates meant to represent in that assembly? In other words, were they sent by

[8] Conc. Constantinop. iii. act. i. (Labbe, t. vii. p. 628), &c.
[9] Labbe, l. c. pp. 942, 972, 1005. προκαθημένου τοῦ εὐσεβεστάτου Ζήνου, &c. [10] Labbe, l. c. p. 1025.
[11] See Leo Allatius De perpetua Consensione Eccl. Occ. et Orient. l. i. c. vi. § v. vi. Coloniæ, p. 94 seq.

the Roman Pontiff in order to learn from the Fathers of Constantinople what doctrine of faith was to be believed? or to enforce the definitions of the Apostolic See, and to procure the solemn confirmation of them by the lawful submission of the Œcumenical Synod? For believers in Papal Infallibility there can be no doubt on this question; and it were to be wished that all Catholics agreed with us in seeing that the mission entrusted to the Legates must have been of the latter nature. The predecessors of Agatho had repeatedly condemned Monothelism, and had anathematised its supporters. In particular Martin I. had already in the Lateran Council defined in the most solemn manner the Catholic teaching concerning the two wills and operations in Christ, and had published his decrees as the standard of faith. To send Papal Legates to the Œcumenical Council in order to discuss anew points of faith which had been already settled, with the intention that they should alter their views, if necessary, according to the new researches to be made in the Council, would have been nothing short of denying Papal Infallibility, by reducing the Universal Doctor of the Church to the rank of any other Bishop, and allowing his solemn judgments of faith to be examined and reformed. But Pope Agatho, like all his predecessors, although he lived six centuries before the complete separation of the East from the West, and ten before the rise of the school of Suarez and Zaccaria, had the firm consciousness of his own infallibility, which he regarded as a doctrine of the whole Catholic Church.

Consequently he sent his Legates with rigorous orders that they should only explain and enforce in the council the traditional doctrine of his Apostolic See, as it had been laid down by his own predecessors.[11] Their mission was not to discuss or examine, as if the matter were doubtful and uncertain, but to set before all in a brief manner the certain and unchangeable doctrine of the Roman See.[12] Pope Agatho gives a reason for these instructions, and this is *the infallibility which had been divinely conferred on the See of Peter.* Therefore he openly asserts that through that supernatural gift his See had always been exempt from any error whatever. On this account he declares that all who wish to save their souls must unanimously profess the formula of faith which rests on the apostolic tradition of Peter, who is the foundation of the Church.[13] Consistently with this, he denounces in the severest terms all who reject this formula, as guilty of a betrayal of the faith, and as deserving a rigorous judgment at the tribunal of Christ.[14] He judges all to be enemies of

[11] "Ut nihil præsumant augere, minuere, vel mutare, sed traditionem hujus Apostolicæ Sedis, ut a prædecessoribus Apostolicis Pontificibus instituta est, sinceriter enarrare." Epist. Agathonis Papæ ad Const. Pogonat. Imp. in act. iv. Conc. Const. iii. (Labbe, t. vii. p. 655.)

[12] "Non tamen tamquam de incertis contendere, sed ut certa atque immutabilia compendiosa definitione proferre." Epist. Agath. Papæ et Syn. Rom. ad Synodum Sextam, in act. iv. conc. vi. (Labbe, l. c. p. 714.)

[13] "Quæ (Ecclesia Rom.) ejus (Petri Apostoli) gratia et præsidio ab omni errore illibata permanet," &c. Epist. Agath. ad Const. Imp. l. c. (Labbe, l. c. p. 698.)

[14] Epist. Agath. cit. l. c. (Labbe, l. c. p. 703.)

the Catholic and Apostolic confession, and subject to perpetual condemnation, who shall refuse to teach the doctrine which he propounds;[15] and over and over again he refers to the infallibility of the Apostolic See as to a pledge and justification of his utterance. He declares that all the orthodox Fathers and all the General Councils had always venerated the teaching of the Roman See, and entirely and faithfully adhered to it; that it had been calumniated and persecuted by none but heretics.[16] He solemnly asserts that it had never at any time declined from the straight path of truth, but that it had always been preserved from error since the Apostles placed in it the deposit of revealed doctrine; and that it should always so last till the end of time, pure and immaculate in its teaching. He alleges in proof of this the promise made by our Lord to Peter, that his faith should never fail.[17] Such is the language with which Pope Agatho and his Synod addressed the Emperor and the Sixth Council. The Roman Pontiff does not expect from the latter a new defini-

[15] Epist. Synod. Agath. cit. l. c. (Labbe, l. c. p. 715.)
[16] Epist. Agath. ad Const. l. c. (Labbe, l. c. p. 659.)
[17] "Quæ (Ecclesia Rom.) ejus (Petri) annitente præsidio nunquam a via veritatis in qualibet erroris parte deflexa est." (Labbe, l. c. p. 659.) "Quæ (Ecclesia Rom.) per Dei Omnipotentis gratiam a tramite Apostolicæ traditionis nunquam errasse probabitur, nec hæreticis novitatibus depravata succubuit, sed ut ab exordio fidei Christianæ percepit ab auctoribus suis Apostolorum Christi Principibus illibata fine tenus permanet, secundum ipsius Domini Salvatoris divinam pollicitationem, quam suorum discipulorum Principi in sacris evangeliis fatus est; Petre, Petre inquiens," &c. (Luc. xxii. 31, 32.) Ib. (Labbe, l. c. p. 662.)

Condemnation of Pope Honorius.

tion of faith. He points out to the Bishops that they should believe and profess, and confirm by their decrees, the traditional infallible doctrine of the Roman See, which all his predecessors had always taught.

The language of Pope Agatho is worthy of a successor of St. Peter, but it in no wise differed from that which the Roman Pontiffs used in other times on such occasions. If we read with attention the letters of Pope Agatho to the Emperor and to the Sixth Synod, and compare them with the time and the circumstances in which they were written, we shall be forced to conclude that they form a summary treatise on the supreme infallible authority of the Apostolic See, considered in its principles and in its practical application. The Oriental Church had fallen into schism because it had allowed itself to be led astray by the subtleties of the Monothelite teachers, and had refused to listen to the infallible voice of the Roman Pontiffs. Now it looked for reconciliation and unity from a Universal Council. Pope Agatho, in his two letters, points out the way to reconciliation and unity. He sets before them the formula of Catholic faith, which is the formula of the Apostolic Magisterium of the Roman See; and he informs them they must believe and confess it, and, on the other hand, condemn and reject every dogma contrary to it. Should they refuse to submit to this rule of faith, they would be in error, in schism, and reprobation. But he could not impose a formula of faith to be believed and confessed unless his Magisterium was universally acknowledged as infallible.

Therefore he repeatedly insists on that capital point of doctrine. He declares that the Roman See has never erred, and that it never shall err. He confirms and explains his assertion by referring to the promises of Christ, to the example of all the Fathers and Doctors of the Church, and of the Œcumenical Synods themselves, which had always received from Rome the paradigm of the doctrine they were to define. At the same time, as supreme and infallible Doctor in the Church, he not only proposes the Catholic formula of faith with regard to the two wills and operations in Christ, but he also exposes the errors of Monothelism, and, by drawing out the traditional doctrine of all the Fathers, he shows the fallacies of the heretics, and affords new weapons for their demolition. Thus we see that the doctrine of the Infallibility of the Roman See is far from being artfully inserted in the Letters of Pope Agatho, as Dr. Döllinger has imagined.[18] This doctrine is woven into their very substance; it is the groundwork of their whole argument. If we make abstraction for a moment from that teaching, the whole drift of the two letters is pointless and meaningless. How could Agatho proclaim an Œcumenical Council to be in error and reprobation, should it decline to receive at his hands the doctrine of faith, had he not been infallible,—had not the doctrine of Papal infallibility been a traditional dogma in the universal Church?

And now let us see how the assembled Fathers received his two letters. Did they lift up their

[18] Op. cit. p. 137.

Condemnation of Pope Honorius. 91

voice in protest against the fundamental doctrine of infallibility which Agatho attributed to his See, and which he rested on the promises of Christ Himself? Was objection raised to the magisterial tone of the letters addressed to an Œcumenical Council? That large and influential assembly of Bishops not only found nothing to censure in the letters of the Pope, but it received them as a whole and in all their parts as if they had been written by St. Peter, or rather by God Himself. The Fathers testified to their admitting the infallible and divine authority of the letters in the eighth session, as well as in the Synodical Letter addressed to Agatho; and in the Prosphonetic Letter sent to the Emperor[19] they regarded them as a rule of faith. No sooner did a suspicion arise that four Bishops and two monks refused to adhere to them, than the Council ordered them to give an explanation of their faith in writing and on oath. They submitted, and solemnly affirmed that they accepted without reserve all the heads of doctrine contained in the letters.[20] Again, Macarius,

---

[19] Conc. Const. iii. act. viii. (Labbe, t. vii. p. 760.) ὡς ἐκ τοῦ Πνεύματος τοῦ Ἁγίου ὑπαγορευθείσας διὰ στόματος τοῦ ἁγίου καὶ κορυφαίου τῶν Ἀποστόλων Πέτρου, καὶ διὰ τοῦ δακτύλου τοῦ προσχόντος τρισμακαρίου πάπα Ἀγάθωνος γραφείας δέχομαι, καὶ συμπνεύσομαι. Epist. Synod. ad Agathonem Papam, in act. xviii. (Labbe, l. c. p. 1109.) ἅτε καὶ ὡς ἀπὸ τῆς κορυφαίας τῶν Ἀποστόλων ἀκρότητος θεολογηθείσα γνώσκομεν. Sermo Prosphoneticus ad Constantinum jam in act. xviii. (Labbe, l. c. p. 1089.) καὶ δι' Ἀγάθωνος ὁ Πέτρος ἐφθέγγετο.

[20] Conc. Const. iii. act. x. (Labbe, l. c. p. 873 sqq.) In the formula presented to the Synod they declared that they adhered simply and without reserve to all the heads of Pope Agatho's letter.

Patriarch of Antioch, was, by sentence of the Council, deposed from his dignity and expelled from the Synod, because he refused to adhere to the letters of Agatho.[21]

The simple truth is, that some of the strongest proofs of Papal Infallibility are found in the acts of this Sixth General Council; so that we may be sure that the objection founded by our adversaries upon the condemnation of Pope Honorius has no solid basis. In order that this objection should have real weight, it must be shown that the Council condemned Honorius as having taught heresy *ex cathedrâ*; but not only is it impossible to give any proof of this, but the contrary may be proved to demonstration. To maintain that the Council condemned Honorius on account of heretical teaching *ex cathedrâ*, is in reality to assert that Pope Agatho and the Synod itself were guilty of the most glaring self-contradiction. Mr. Renouf admits that "the papal legates, who were strictly tied by their instructions, must have had Pope Agatho's consent to the condemnation of Honorius." But since there is no trace in his letters of his having given such consent, Mr. Renouf concludes that they must have had secret instructions.[22] So, according to Mr. Renouf, Pope Agatho must have on the one hand solemnly taught in his letters to the Emperors and to the Synod, that his predecessors had never erred, nor could be led into error, founded as they were on the solid rock of

---

[21] Conc. Const. iii. act. viii. (Labbe, l. c. p. 768.)
[22] The Condemnation of Pope Honorius, p. 17.

the divine promises, while on the other hand he gave secret instructions to his legates to condemn Honorius precisely for having taught heresy *ex cathedrâ!* Would not such conduct have contained at one and the same time the folly of self-contradiction and the shame of dishonesty? With regard to the Council, it had repeatedly acknowledged all the heads of doctrine mentioned in Pope Agatho's letter. By adhering to it the Synod had professed that none of the predecessors of Agatho had ever erred, being founded on the rock of Peter, and deriving security from the promises of Christ; implicitly, therefore, it had made a solemn profession that Honorius, being a Pope, had not taught any heresy *ex cathedrâ*. How could it, then, at that very time, condemn him as having taught heresy to the universal Church? Especially as even after the condemnation of Honorius the Fathers show that they had not forgotten the doctrine to which they gave their adherence by adopting Pope Agatho's letter. In the Synodical Address in which they inform the Pope of all the proceedings of the Council, and in particular of the condemnation of the heretics and of Honorius himself, they solemnly acknowledge the authority of the Papal letters, as if they were written by the Apostle Peter himself; and on this account they leave it to the Pope to decide what is to be done in defence of the faith, because, they say, he rests on the firm rock of faith.[23] In the Prosphonetic Letter to the Emperor Constantine they

[23] Litteræ sextæ Synodi ad Agathonem Papam, act. xviii. (Labbe, l. c. p. 1109.)

inculcate the same doctrine, and declare that Peter himself spoke through Agatho.[24] In these passages we read the authentic commentary of the Synod itself upon its own act in condemning Honorius. The Council consistently maintains throughout the doctrine of Papal Infallibility; wherefore, in condemning Honorius, it could not have meant that he had taught heresy *ex cathedrâ*. No council ever committed itself to so flagrant a contradiction and so disgraceful a deceit. Again, the Synod professed to receive Agatho's letters as divinely written, so that they received them as containing doctrines based on Divine revelation; it is, therefore, incredible that the Council solemnly decreed anything the truth of which would prove that the divine promises were falsified. Pope Agatho, moreover, said to the Council in his letters: " The Roman See has never erred, and never will err, because of Christ's promise." The assembled Fathers answered: " This, as well as the other doctrinal teachings of his letters, is the teaching of St. Peter." And they spoke in this tone, not only before the condemnation of Honorius, but also after it, in the final Synodical Letter sent by them in the last session to Pope Agatho, and in the Prosphonetic Address to the Emperor. On all these grounds it is absurd to think that the Council condemned Honorius for having taught heresy in the Church. Our adversaries not only charge the Council with self-contradiction, but also with having fallen into a most

---

[24] See the Prosphonetic Letter addressed to the Emperor, in act. xviii. (Labbe, l. c. p. 1089.)

grievous doctrinal error. A Pope and an Œcumenical Council joined in the profession that a certain doctrine was true and divine; and yet it is maintained that they afterwards rejected that doctrine! This they could not do without abandoning their own character for infallibility. Here we see the reason why the Sixth Synod applied the word "dogmatic" to the letters of Agatho;[25] while they never use that epithet of the letters of Honorius. Mr. Renouf passes over all these points; and after having quoted from Bellarmine a remark upon the subject, he leaves it to "the partisans of the culpable remissness of Honorius to settle this question with Bellarmine."[26] This is a very unfair and shuffling manner of shaking off the weight of a strong objection.

What, then, was really the offence for which Pope Honorius was condemned by the Sixth Synod? This is a question of great interest, not because the doctrine of Papal Infallibility depends upon it, but because the answer strikes at the very root of the objections raised by our adversaries against the purity of faith of that Pope. We have several passages in the Acts of the Sixth Council in which Pope Honorius is either decried or spoken of. In three of them Honorius is condemned apart from the Monothelite heretics, and distinct causes are mentioned for the condemnation of him and for that of the others; while in three other places he is condemned in common with

[25] See the Prosphonetic Letter addressed to the Emperor, in act. xviii. (Labbe, l. c. p. 1088.)
[26] Renouf, l. c. pp. 17, 18.

the rest. The three former passages are to be found in the Decree of Condemnation, in the Prosphonetic Letter, and in the Imperial Edict.[27] The others may be seen at the end of the thirteenth session, in the Definition, and in the Synodical Letter to Pope Agatho; to these the first part also of the Decree may be added.[28] Now it is clear that the latter class of passages ought to be explained by the former, because, among other reasons, it contains the actual Decree of Condemnation, on which is founded whatever else is said concerning Honorius.

Let us first examine this important document. In a note we give the decree in the Latin version,[29]

[27] Labbe, l. c. pp. 977, 1089, 1121.
[28] Ib. pp. 1005, 1057, 1109, 977.
[29] "Retractantes dogmaticas epistolas, quæ tanquam a Sergio quondam Patr. hujus a Deo conservandæ regiæ urbis scriptæ sunt, tam ad Cyrum, qui tunc fuerat episcopus Phasidis, quam ad Honorium quondam papam antiquæ Romæ: similiter autem et epistolam ab illo, id est Honorio, rescriptam ad eundem Sergium; hasque invenientes omnino alienas existere ab Apostolicis dogmatibus, et a definitionibus sanctorum conciliorum et cunctorum probabilium Patrum, sequi vero falsas doctrinas hæreticorum, eas omnino abjicimus et tanquam animæ noxias execramur. Quorum autem, id est eorundem impia execramur dogmata, horum et nomina a sancta Dei Ecclesia projici judicavimus, id est Sergii . . . . qui aggressus est de hujusmodi impio dogmate conscribere, Cyri Alexandrini, Pyrrhi, Petri et Pauli, qui et ipsi præsulatu fancti sunt in sede hujus a Deo conservandæ civitatis, et similia eis senserunt, ad hæc et Theodori quondam episcopi Pharan, quarum omnium suprascriptarum personarum mentionem fecit Agatho sanctissimus ac ter beatissimus Papa antiquæ Romæ in suggestione, quam fecit ad piissimum et a Deo confirmatum Dominum nostrum et magnum imperatorem, eosque abjicit, utpote contraria rectæ fidei nostræ sentientes, quos anathemati submitti definimus. Cum his vero simul projici a sancta Dei catholica ecclesia simulque anathematizari præ-

and from it it is clear that the Council purposely draws a line of distinction between the cause of Sergius, Cyrus, Pyrrhus, Paul, Peter, Theodore, with others who agreed with them,—and that of Honorius. Of the former it is said; "these are the names of those whose impious doctrines we execrate :" the names *i.e.* of those whom Pope Agatho mentioned in his letters, and condemned as professing doctrines contrary to the faith ; and, in conformity with Agatho's sentence, they pronounce anathema on them. It is evident, then, that Sergius and the rest were condemned as heretics. But Honorius is spoken of apart from them, and the Synod declares that he is anathematised because in all things he followed Sergius, and gave strength to the impious doctrines: "quia in omnibus ejus (Sergii) mentem sequutus est, et impia dogmata confirmavit."[80] No one believed that the Pope had taught the impious doctrines which were execrated, or even that he had held them internally. And accordingly no expression to this effect was used concerning him either in the Prosphonetic Letter to Constantine, or in the edict of the Emperor. In the first of these two documents the Fathers called the Monothelite Eastern Patriarchs *inventors* of heretical novelties ; but as to Honorius they used

---

vidimus et Honorium, qui fuerat papa antiquæ Romæ, eo quod invenimus per scripta quæ ab eo facta sunt ad Sergium, quod in omnibus ejus mentem sequutus est et impia dogmata confirmavit." In act. xiii. Conc. vi. (Labbe, l. c.)

[80] κατὰ πάντα τῇ ἐκείνου γνώμῃ ἐξακολουθήσαντα, καὶ τὰ αὐτοῦ ἀσιβῆ κυρώσαντα δόγματα. l. c.

the very expression of the decree, since they say of him "qui eos in his sequutus est."[31] In the others Honorius is termed "hujus hæreseos confirmator, qui etiam sui extitit oppugnator."[32] Now what does the Council mean by τῇ γνώμῃ ἐξακολουθήσαντα? We have already answered this question in the preceding section. Sergius, indeed, applied to Pope Honorius in order to have a sanction to the economy of silence with regard to the expression one or two operations in Christ; and although he artfully insinuated the maxims of Monothelism, still he showed no open anxiety for anything but to obtain the papal confirmation for his scheme of economical silence. And what adherence did Honorius give in his answer to Sergius? Certainly he gave no adherence to the heresy; for the doctrine expressed in his letters is wholly Catholic, and entirely contrary to that expressed by Sergius. But he consented without any limitation to the economy of silence proposed by the Patriarch. In this then, and in nothing else, did he follow Sergius' mind (τῇ γνώμῃ ἐξακολουθήσαντα); and τῇ γνώμῃ can here mean nothing but 'scheme.'

Honorius, in truth, was not guilty of any error in his apprehension of doctrine, as were the other prelates condemned as heretics by the Synod: his error was practical, and consisted only in the economy of silence by which he favoured the development of the heresy, and allowed it to strike deep

[31] Sermo Prosphoneticus, l. c. ὡς ἐκείνως ἐν τούτοις ἀκολουθήσαντα.
[32] Edictum, l. c.

and extensive root. It is true that, as appears from his letters, he did not see in that practical economy anything counter to the faith, especially as no Council had yet definitively fixed the language suitable to express the dogma of the wills and operations in Christ. But he did not seek advice from any Roman Synod; he did not inquire into the true course of recent events in the Eastern provinces; he did not obtain reliable information on the character of those prelates who were so anxious to impose silence on the most zealous champions of Catholic truth. His acquaintance both with persons and things was evidently most imperfect; and this aggravates his fault; for he kept silence when he should have raised his Apostolical voice against the promoters of heresy, and brought them back to the Catholic confession, or if this failed, anathematised them, and checked their attempts to corrupt the faith. But why did he abstain from censuring and condemning the errors insinuated in the letters of Sergius, and defended by Cyrus and the others? Satisfied with having stated in his answers the pure doctrine of the Church, he passed over without any notice the destructive errors which were contained in those letters, and even insisted on the economy of silence, which proved a weapon of great power in the hands of the Monothelite leaders against the Catholic teaching. We repeat, the enemies of the faith never once sought to obtain from Honorius any consent to their errors; they wanted nothing more than the economical silence, that they might labour undisturbed at the ruin of the Catholic doctrine. Honorius, in violation of every principle of ecclesiastical prudence, granted what they asked. Here was his fault. Whatever his intention may have been, he fully adhered to the proposal of Sergius, by which the heresy was confirmed and took deeper root in the East. Therefore is he said in the decree to have confirmed the impious dogma of the Patriarch, and in the edict of Constantine he is called "confirmer of the Monothelite heresy." But at the same time the Synod neither attributed to him the invention of the new heresy, nor any adhesion to it; and in the edict it is pointedly said that he "etiam sui extitit oppugnator;" because, whilst by his fatal economy of silence he contributed to strengthen and spread the new heresy, he, at the same time, advocated the true Catholic doctrine concerning the two operations in Christ.

Mr. Renouf attaches great importance to the word κυρώσαντα of the decree. "The Sixth Œcumenical Council," he says, "expressly condemns Honorius as κυρώσαντα the impious dogmas of Sergius, having officially confirmed and ratified them, and stamped them with authority." And he adds that "lexicographers tell us, κυρῶσαι non tam significare comprobare, quam cum auctoritate decernere, legitime rem transigere, ut demum ratum sit quod actum fuerit."[83] Now Mr. Renouf should be reminded first that Stephanus, to whom he refers, adds, after the quoted words, "subjungitur tamen l.

[83] The Condemnation of Pope Honorius, p. 23.

Herod, in quo simpliciter redditur verbo *confirmare*."[84] And again, even if the word κυρώσαντα should be taken to signify a confirmation with authority, its application must be to a consequence of Honorius having followed the mind of Sergius. Honorius, indeed, instead of using his apostolical authority in checking and condemning the new heresy, used it wrongly in enforcing the economy of silence as proposed by Sergius. Thus in fact and historically, so to speak, his authority was used in confirmation and propagation of the very heresy which he intended to suppress. Mr. Renouf is wrong in attributing to the word κυρώσαντα any such meaning as affects Honorius' understanding and will. On the contrary, whilst we admit, by way of concession, the signification of an authoritative confirmation, we free the Pope from the charge of a fault which would have been a glaring contradiction with the tenets he expresses in his letters.

To proceed now to the language used by the Synod in the other passages where Honorius is condemned, together with the others; we unhesitatingly say that it no way opposes the view we take. For since Honorius, by his imprudent economy of silence and his grievous neglect in the discharge of his duties, contributed to the spread of the new heresy, he partook of the same fault *in solidum* with the others, although he had not himself been guilty of any heresy whatever; and such language is quite in accordance

---

[84] Stephani Thesaurus, t. iv. p. 5476, ad vocem κυρώσαι. Londini, 1822.

with the technical and canonical language used by the Church.[35] We need not wonder then, if in the definition of faith the Pope is joined with the other Monothelites, and called an instrument of the devil, who availed himself of it to spread the new errors;[36] if, in the synodical letter to Agatho the Fathers say that they have slain with their anathemas Honorius, with the Eastern prelates, as sinners in a matter of faith;[37] if in the thirteenth session his letters, in common with the writings of the heretics, are condemned to be burned as soul-destroying, and contributing to the same crime.[38] Pope Honorius did in truth, by his false economy and his neglect, become an instrument of the devil against the faith; therefore he was guilty of betrayal of the faith, and, in a way different to the rest, he contributed to the same iniquity,—that is to say, to the propagation of the heresy and the destruction of souls. In the same manner, in the first part of the decree, Honorius' letters, as well as the writings of the others, are called "alien from the apostolic teachings, following the false teachings of the heretics, and soul-destroying." But although these expressions, taken in a general way, are all suitable *in solidum*, they cannot be referred to Honorius' letters in the same sense in which they concern those of Sergius, Theodore, Pyrrhus, and other heretical authors. In the strict

---

[35] See Epist. xxi. Cœlestini Papæ ad Episcopos Galliarum, n. 2. (Constant. Epist. Rom. Pontif. p. 1186.)

[36] Act. xviii. Conc. vi. (Labbe, l. c. p. 1057.)

[37] Ib. (Labbe, l. c. p. 1109.)   [38] Labbe, l. c. p. 1005.

sense, they relate only to the latter; as is borne out by the second part of the decree, which we have just examined. The letters of Honorius are truly alien from the apostolic teachings, not because they contain any error contrary to the traditional doctrines handed down by the Apostles, but because they do not reveal that ecclesiastical prudence and diligence, that courage in correcting erroneous doctrines and reducing the minds of heretics to obedience, which have always been traditional in the Church, and ever practised by the Roman Pontiffs. The letters followed the false teachings of the heretics,—that is to say, they helped and supported the false teachings of the heretics (ἱσομένας).[89] Sergius and the others, by their writings, helped and supported heresy, because they adopted and directly promoted the spread of false doctrine; Honorius did so, only because, by his fatal economy of silence, he helped that teaching to be spread and gain strength.

We wonder that Mr. Renouf ascribes so great importance to the testimony given by the Patriarchs Pyrrhus and Macarius against the purity of Honorius' faith. Undoubtedly two Monothelite prelates could not well speak differently; they could not appeal for support to Honorius' successors, who had openly and solemnly condemned their errors. But Honorius, by his false economy of silence, had already compromised his character, and opened the

---

[89] The deponent middle verb ἵσμαι in its fundamental signification means not only to follow, but hence also to stand by, to help, to support.

door to calumny. However, although it is true that Pyrrhus and Macarius charged Honorius with heresy, yet the Council never intended to condemn him as a heretic. Neither can our adversaries sustain any objection founded upon the words of the Synod addressed to Pope Agatho, when they declare that they have slain with anathema those who were guilty in a matter of faith (περὶ τὴν πίστιν ἡμαρτηκότας), according to the sentence previously issued by Agatho against them in his second letter.

In addition to the remarks which we have already made on this passage, it may be here observed that the above words do not properly concern Pope Honorius. The allusion to the decree of the thirteenth session, which concerns only the Monothelite prelates, and the words in question, follow close after the sentence of condemnation of these prelates, in which, as we saw above, Honorius is not comprehended. The Council, after having mentioned the names of Sergius, Cyrus, Theodore of Pharan, Pyrrhus, Peter, and Paul, whose impious dogmas it execrates, continues: "quarum omnium suprascriptarum personarum mentionem fecit Agatho sanctissimus et ter beatissimus Papa antiquæ Romæ in suggestione quam fecit ad piissimum et a Deo confirmatum dominum nostrum et magnum imperatorem."[40] It is certain that Pope Agatho mentioned no other names except those of the heretics: neither in his letter to the Emperor, nor in the letter addressed to the Synod, did he allude to any one else—much less to Honorius, who,

[40] Act. xiii. (Labbe, l. c. p. 978.)

Condemnation of Pope Honorius.

as we said above, was certainly spoken of in his letter as one of his predecessors, who had endeavoured to defend the Catholic doctrine by imposing silence on the Monothelite leaders. On this account, in the synodical address to Pope Agatho, the Fathers made distinct mention of those who had been pointed out in that Pope's letters, and of Macarius and Polychronius, who, although not mentioned by the Pope, had been slain as heretics with their anathemas. Pope Honorius did not properly belong either to the first class or to the second. But the Synod, in its summary report to the Pope, divided the anathematised persons into those who had departed this life and those who were still living,[41] and it classed Honorius with the former, although he had not partaken in the same manner of their iniquity. At all events, the decree of condemnation inserted in the thirteenth session would have been sufficient to point out the nature of his crime. It is true, however, that the Sixth Synod did not examine the cause of Honorius, nor pronounce sentence against him, without the previous authorisation of the Roman See. Otherwise its proceedings would have been unlawful, according to the maxim expressed by Pope Adrian II. in his third Allocution to the eighth Œcumenical Council.[42]

But we must consider whether the Roman See

---

[41] "Post eos, anathematibus haereticorum juste subjecimus et eos qui vivunt, suscepta illorum impietate," &c. (Labbe, l. c. p. 1110.)

[42] Conc. Constantinop. iv. act. vii. (Labbe, t. x. p. 597.)

authorised the Fathers of the Sixth Synod to condemn Honorius as a heretic. Mr. Renouf sets great value on the acclamations of the sixteenth session,[43] in which *anathema* was said *to Honorius the heretic*, as it was to the others who had been previously condemned by the Council in the thirteenth session. On this we remark, first, that the acclamation quoted not only is no definitive sentence, but does not even show what was the feeling of the whole Council. In the sixteenth session, after the condemnation of Constantine a priest of Apamea in Syria, George the Patriarch of Constantinople declared to the assembled Fathers that he and some others among the Bishops dependent on him were anxious that the Synod, through economy (δι' οἰκονομίαν), should, if possible, abstain from anathematising any person by name (ὀνομαστί) in their acclamations,—as, for instance, Sergius, Pyrrhus, Paul, and Peter.[44] If he asked for this kind of condescension in his own name, as well as in that of other Bishops, in favour of the authors of the new heresy, because of their having been Patriarchs of Constantinople, much more must they have intended that no such expression should be used in the case of Honorius, who was not the originator of the error. But the majority of the Synod refused to follow the suggestion of economy, and resolved to anathematise by name all those who were already condemned (τοὺς καταχρί-

---

[43] Ὁνωρίῳ αἱρετικῷ ἀνάθεμα (Labbe, l. c. p. 1044). Mr. Renouf has even printed these words on the cover of his pamphlet!
[44] Conc. vi. act. xvi. (Labbe, l. c. p. 1044.)

τους). It follows that all persons mentioned in the acclamations were to be designated in accordance with the previous decree of their condemnation. Now we have seen that in the decree Honorius was not condemned on account of any heretical tenet. Why, then, it will be asked, is he termed "heretic" in the acclamations? Two explanations may be given. Either the Synod, by applying this term to Honorius without qualification, used it in its secondary meaning, according to the opinion of many learned theologians, confirmed by several examples in antiquity,[45]—or it is to be attributed to a faction, which, like that of Gerson in the Synod of Constance, contrived to vent all its bitterness against Honorius in the final synodical acclamations. We must admit the existence of such a Greek faction in the Sixth Synod, which it was impossible to keep in thorough control on account of the absence of the Western Prelates. "Honorius," said Adrian II., "was anathematised by the Orientals."[46] This remark of Adrian II. deserves attention. We have already admitted the fault of Pope Honorius, and the justice of the sentence pronounced against him. But still we must confess that we feel far greater admiration for the Fathers of the Lateran Council,—belonging for the most part to the West,—who behaved as dutiful children in concealing their father's

---

[45] See, for instance, Suarez De Fide, disp. xxiv. sect. 1. n. 6. "Omissive autem censetur favere (hæresi), qui omittit facere quod tenetur, ut hæreticus puniatur vel ab errore cesset."

[46] Allocutio tertia Hadriani ad Synodum viii. (Labbo, t. x. p. 597.)

shame, than for the Greek Bishops of the Sixth Synod, who gave the first example in the Church of so solemn a condemnation of a Pope. At all events, we cannot help strongly denouncing the exaggeration and bitterness of expression used in his condemnation: these are certainly due to a faction,—a strong faction,—which exercised its influence in that Council, and carried the day. It is in such facts that we see the reason why the acts of all synods are under the control of the Supreme Pastor and Ruler of the Church. Even if all the Prelates of the East had joined in condemning Honorius as a heretic (which we deny), their decree would have been without authority in the Church, unless it were sealed with the mark of the Sovereign Pontiff. On this point there is no difference of opinion between Gallicans and the rest of Catholics, whom Mr. Renouf is pleased to call Ultramontane. The assembly of the Bishops cannot represent the Church unless it is in close union with the Pope; and therefore its decrees cannot have authority unless stamped with the authority of the Pope himself. On this account it is idle to pick out of the acts of the Sixth Synod expressions and phrases aggravating the sentence of condemnation against Pope Honorius. The main question is well put by Dr. Ward, in his article in the *Dublin Review* on Mr. Renouf's pamphlet: "What declarations of the Council against Honorius received Pontifical sanction, and in what sense they received it."[47]

It is true that Pope Leo II., who succeeded

[47] Dublin Review, July 1868, p. 217.

Condemnation of Pope Honorius. 109

Agatho in the Pontifical See, confirmed the Third Council of Constantinople, and ranked it with the Œcumenical Synods; but what decrees of the Sixth Synod received his supreme sanction, and in what sense did they receive it? The Fathers of the Sixth Synod, at the end of the eighteenth session, asked the Emperor to send to all the patriarchal Sees an authentic copy of the definition of faith, signed by the Council (ἰσοτύπους ἐνυπογράφους ὅρους).[48] Pope Leo II. confirmed nothing but the definition of faith, although he received all the acts of the Synod, together with the imperial edict. We have several letters of this Pope in which he either authoritatively confirms the Sixth Council, or communicates to the Bishops his adhesion to it. In all and each of them he pointedly limits his confirmation and approval to the dogmatic definition. In his official letter to the Emperor he declares only that he confirms the definition of the right faith (τῆς ὀρθῆς πίστεως τὸν ὅρον).[49] In his letter to the Bishops of Spain he tells them that he forwards to them the definition of faith sanctioned in the Sixth Synod, the prosphonetic address to the Emperor, and his edict; he promises that he will send the whole of the conciliar acts; but he requires their signatures to no more than the definition of faith.[50] He says

---

[48] Labbe, t. vii. p. 1108.
[49] Exemplar Relationis missæ a Leone Papa ad Constantinum Imp. (Labbe, t. vii. p. 1153.)
[50] Epist. ii. Leonis II. ad Episcopos Hispaniæ (Labbe, t. vii. p. 1456-57). "Ab omnibus reverendis Episcopis una vobiscum subscriptionis in eadem definitione venerandi concilii subnectantur."

the same in his letter to Simplicius,[51] and in that addressed to King Ervigius.[52] So that no doubt whatever can remain with regard to his intention being really what he expresses. Again, in what manner did he sanction the definition of faith, and in what sense did he anathematise Honorius? "Since the holy, universal, and great Sixth Synod," he says, ... "has followed in everything the apostolic doctrine of the most eminent Fathers, and since it preached the same definition of the right faith, which the Apostolic See of the holy Apostle Peter received with veneration, therefore we, and through our exercise of our office this venerable Apostolic See, gives full consent to the things contained in the definition of faith, and confirms them with the authority of the blessed Peter, that, being placed on the solid rock of Christ Himself, it may be supplied by the Lord with strength."[53]

The main reason, therefore, why Pope Leo sanctions the definition of the right faith is, because he found it conformable to the doctrine of the Pontifical See, by which the Synod itself, as it had already confessed, had been instructed.[54] Hence he exhibited

[51] Epist. iv. Leonis II. ad Simplicium Comitem (Labbe, l. c. p. 1460). "Hortati autem sumus reverendissimos ecclesiarum omnium præsules, ut subscriptiones suas eidem apostolicæ synodali definitioni subnectant."

[52] Epist. v. Leonis II. ad Ervigium regem Hispaniæ (Labbo, l. c. p. 1462).

[53] Relatio cit. Leonis II. ad Constantinum Imp. (Labbe, l. c. p. 1153.)

[54] ἐμεῖς τῷ ἁγίῳ πνεύματι λαμπρυνόμενοι, καὶ ταῖς ὑμετέραις διδασ-

the Pontifical See as the authentic organ of the apostolical teaching. It was not enough that the doctrine contained in the definition had gone along with the doctrine of the Fathers; it was necessary that it should concur with the teaching of the Apostolic See; for the doctrine of the Fathers is a stream from that head-fountain. But if the truth of a dogmatic doctrine depends upon its agreeing with the teaching of the Pontifical See, we have here plain evidence of the infallibility of that See in its doctrinal Magisterium. Pope Leo II. therefore, no less than Agatho his predecessor, upheld the doctrine of Pontifical Infallibility in the act by which he sanctioned the dogmatical definition of the Sixth Council. Consequently he implicitly declared that whatever was the character of the fault of Honorius, it was certainly not that of having taught any error *ex cathedrâ*.

Once more: what sanction did Leo II. give to the condemnation of Honorius in common with the Bishops of the Monothelite faction, which is to be found in the definition of faith? In his letter of confirmation of the Sixth Council addressed to the Emperor Constantine, after having anathematised the earlier heretics, he continues: "Likewise we anathematise the inventors of the new error: Theodore Bishop of Pharan, Cyrus of Alexandria, Sergius, Pyrrhus, Paul, Peter, traitors rather than rulers of the Church of Constantinople. Moreover,

---

καλαῖς ὁδηγούμενοι, &c. Epist. Synodal. ad Agathonem Papam, in act. xviii. (Labbe, t. vii. p. 1112.)

Honorius also, who did not endeavour to preserve pure the Apostolic Church by the doctrine of the apostolic tradition, but permitted (παρεχώρησι) the Immaculate to be defiled by profane betrayal."⁵⁵

Before making our remarks on this passage, we must revert for a moment to Mr. Renouf. This gentleman makes a small addition to Pope Leo's words, and bases on this additional word his answer to the argument derived from the passage. "A passage of Pope Leo II.," he writes, "is also appealed to, in which he says that Honorius '*permitted* the immaculate Church to be polluted by his profane betrayal.' I cannot see how this saves Honorius."⁵⁶ It is undeniable that the passage construed as Mr. Renouf construes it cannot save Honorius; his cause is lost if he permitted the Church to be polluted by *his* profane betrayal. But Mr. Renouf did not find in the text, whether Greek or Latin, that pronoun *his* which he gratuitously adds in his translation of the original. It does not exist either in the Greek or in the old Latin translation, or even in Dr. Döllinger's *Papstbuch über Honorius*.⁵⁷ If the pronoun be rejected, which has thus been uncritically and unjustifiably inserted, the Greek text easily and without the slightest strain yields a good sense.⁵⁸

⁵⁵ Relatio cit. Leonis II. ad Const. Imp. (Labbe, L c. p. 1156.)
⁵⁶ The Condemnation, &c. p. 13 n.   ⁵⁷ Papst Fabeln, p. 138.
⁵⁸ Peter De Marca, in his time, saw no difficulty in the Greek text, and he translated it as follows : "qui Apostolicam Ecclesiam non est conatus lustrare doctrina apostolicæ traditionis, sed profana præditione puram maculari permisit." In Vita Petri De Marca scripta a Balutio, p. 29.

Condemnation of Pope Honorius. 113

For the present we shall say nothing about the similarity which Mr. Renouf finds between the passage in question and the second profession of faith made by the Roman Pontiffs, as it exists in the *Liber Diurnus*. Returning, then, to the words of Pope Leo, it clearly follows from them that Honorius was not condemned for heresy, but because, through his negligence, he permitted the heretics to spread in the East the error of one will and operation in Christ. Pope Leo drew a line of demarcation between the Monothelite Prelates and Pope Honorius: he described the former as *inventors* of the new error (τοὺς ἐξευρετὰς τῆς νέας πλάνης); but he placed the fault of the latter in a grievous neglect in the discharge of his pontifical duties, for which the immaculate Church was *allowed* to be polluted by profane betrayal (τῇ βιβήλῳ προδοσίᾳ). These last words evidently refer to the Monothelite Prelates, inventors of the new error, and they by no means concern Honorius. It is impossible to refer them to him; for he could not be said to have permitted the immaculate Church to be polluted, when he had so acted as to pollute it in a direct manner by his profane betrayal.

In the other two letters addressed by the same Pontiff to the Bishops of Spain and to King Ervigius, he does not make use of expressions calculated to mitigate the force of the condemnation of Honorius, but he explains what he had already expressed in the letter to the Emperor: so that the three letters put together exhibit in full the view

I

taken by Pope Leo of the case. In the former he again draws a marked distinction between the Monothelite Prelates and Honorius: the former are called "perduelliones adversum apostolicæ traditionis puritatem;" and this is the crime to which their condemnation is ascribed, namely, the crime of heresy. Pope Leo does not, as Mr. Renouf ventures to say, include Honorius among the "perduelliones adversum apostolicæ traditionis puritatem."[59] The Pontiff clearly and explicitly alleges the cause of his condemnation, making it quite distinct from that of the heretics; and he rests it on the omission to extinguish at its outset the flame of the heretical error, as required by the dignity of the apostolic authority, and on the negligence which fostered it.[60] These expressions, no less than those of the letter to the Emperor, do not give any hint whatever of Honorius having privately adhered to the Monothelite heresy, or of his having preached it, and having been condemned for it. Again, in the other letter to King Ervigius, Leo II. did not speak of Honorius to any different effect. Nevertheless Mr. Renouf attaches far greater importance to Leo's words in this letter, as supporting his opinion, than is done by any other writer on the same side; and he is surprised that Dr. Döllinger seems not to have

[59] The Condemnation, &c. p. 5.

[60] "Qui flammam hæretici dogmatis, non ut decuit apostolicam auctoritatem, incipientem extinxit, sed negligendo confovit." Epistola ii. Leonis II. ad Episcopos Hispaniæ (Labbe, t. vii. p. 1156).

recognised their force.⁶¹ But the Munich professor is so far from laying any stress whatever on the passage in question, that he is inclined to think its expressions are calculated to soften down the impression produced by the condemnation of Honorius. What, then, is the reason why Mr. Renouf makes so much of Leo's words? Speaking of Pope Leo he says, "he includes Honorius among the *omnes hi* who, *unam voluntatem unamque operationem prædicantes, doctrinam hæreticam impudenter defendere conabantur*."⁶² This assertion is altogether erroneous, and so evidently erroneous that no one of all the adversaries of Honorius ever dreamt of founding an objection on this passage; but, on the contrary, all of them regard Leo's letter to King Ervigius as an objection to their theory. Pope Leo indeed, in this as well as in the other places quoted above, draws a broad line between the Monothelite Bishops and Pope Honorius. He terms the former "authors of heretical assertion,"⁶³ as in the letter to the Spanish Bishops. Of Honorius he says, that he was anathematised *una cum eis;* but he evidently denies that he

⁶¹ See Mr. Renouf's Letter, of June 20, 1868, to the Westminster Gazette.

⁶² The Condemnation of Pope Honorius, p. 5, and the Letter quoted in the preceding note.

⁶³ The whole passage is as follows: "Omnes hæreticæ assertionis auctores, venerando consento concilio condemnati, de Catholicæ Ecclesiæ adunatione projecti sunt, id est, Theodorus Pharanitanus episcopus, Cyrus Alexandrinus, Sergius, Paulus, et Petrus, quondam Constantinopolitani præsules, et una cum eis Honorius Romanus, qui immaculatam apostolicæ traditionis regulam, quam

was condemned for the same reason. Had he thought that Honorius was to be included among the "auctores hæreticæ assertionis," as one of them, he would have put down his name with the others under the same category, before or immediately following Paul, Pyrrhus, and Peter: if he meant this, then *una cum eis* was no way required. But the Pope's meaning is, that Honorius was associated with the rest in being condemned, but not in the crime for which they were condemned; and therefore it was necessary to use a connecting phrase to make it known that Honorius was not placed in every respect on a par with the heretics condemned by the Council. In fact, Leo immediately goes on to mention the cause of the condemnation of Honorius, saying, "qui immaculatam apostolicæ traditionis regulam, quam a prædecessoribus suis accepit, maculari consensit."a These words render exactly the same idea as is conveyed by the extracts quoted above from the other two letters of Leo, and together with them they prove to demonstration that Pope Leo characterised the fault of Honorius in such a way as to exclude even the slightest adhesion on his part to any error whatever. Now, reverting to Mr. Renouf's objection, we argue as follows: Pope Leo includes among the

---

a prædecessoribus suis accepit, maculari consensit; sed et Macarium, &c. .... et omnes hi cum Ario, Apollinario, &c. .... unam voluntatem unamque operationem prædicantes, doctrinam hæreticam impudenter defendere conabantur." Epist. v. Leonis II. ad Ervigium (Labbe, l. c. p. 1462).

"*omnes hi*, qui, unam voluntatem unamque operationem prædicantes, doctrinam hæreticam impudenter defendere conabantur," all those who had been "hæreticæ assertionis auctores." But he evidently excludes from this class Pope Honorius; therefore he does not include him among the *omnes hi*. Had he intended to do so, he would have contradicted his own assertion; because he could not say that Honorius had consented to the defilement of the rule of the apostolic tradition, if that Pope had been one of those who endeavoured impudently to advocate an heretical doctrine. Mr. Renouf's confusion of thought on this point is inexplicable.

As to the *Liber Diurnus*, we are at a loss to comprehend the stress Mr. Renouf lays on it as the best support of his attack on Pope Honorius. The learned Garnier, who was the first to publish a perfect edition of that book, writes as follows in the preface:[64] "Cur tandem prodent [*Liber Diurnus*] fecit hæc una, vel sola, vel potissima causa, ut motam de Honorio quæstionem, magnaque animorum contentione non tam agitatam, quam vexatam, ostenderem ita componi posse, vel ipso centum fere summorum Pontificum judicio, ut neque Sedis Apostolicæ, cujus meum colendæ studium nulli velim esse impar, fides nunquam vitiata dicatur; neque incredibiles fingantur actorum Sextæ Synodi aliorumque veterum monumentorum corruptionis, quod et historica doctrina mirum quantum abhorret; neque Sexta Synodus, cui

[64] Liber Diurnus RR. PP. opera et studio J. Garnerii S.J. præfatio, ed. Migne, t. cv. PP. LL. p. 12.

legati Sedis Apostolicæ præfuerint, erroris arguatur; neque Honorius, quamvis omnino fuerit pravus, Monothelismi culpâ caruisse putandus sit."

"The principal and only reason for which the *Liber Diurnus* is at length published, is, that the controversy on Honorius, which has been so long agitated, may be finally so settled by the judgment of nearly one hundred Sovereign Pontiffs, that no doubt may remain as to the truth that the faith of the Apostolic See has never been defiled; that strange corruptions may no longer be introduced into the acts of the Sixth Synod, and other ancient monuments, in opposition to every principle of historical criticism; that no charge of error may be sustainable against the Sixth Synod, in which legates of the Apostolic See presided; and that while Honorius is purged of the charge of Monothelism, he may not be deemed guiltless of all fault."

Thus Garnier shows that not only does the *Liber Diurnus* furnish documents which cast light on the whole question of the Sixth Council, and of the condemnation of Honorius, but also it affords materials for the defence of that Pope against the charge of heresy brought by his calumniators.

But there is more to be said. When the Archbishop De Marca was preparing to compose a dissertation in defence of Pope Honorius, his friend Labbe sent to him an extract from the MS. copy of the *Liber Diurnus*, on which De Marca set much value, and which he determined to insert in his Apology, with the other extracts which he had already gathered together.⁶⁵ It might seem incredible that the same passage which De Marca regarded as so valuable for the defence, is the very one which Mr. Renouf, following in the steps of Dr. Döllinger,⁶⁶ produces as an important part of the case against that Pope!⁶⁷

The passage is found in the second profession of faith, of which Gregory II. seems to be the author (715-731). It runs as follows: "Auctores vero novi hæretici dogmatis [anathematizamus], Sergium, Pyrrhum, Paulum, et Petrum Constantinopolitanos, una cum Honorio, qui pravis eorum assertionibus fomentum impendit."⁶⁸ It is impossible to help seeing that these words do not imply any more than the foregoing extracts from Leo's letters. The fact is that the character of being author of the new heretical dogma is not attributed to Honorius, but only to Sergius and the others. Honorius is condemned and anathematised with them, but not because he was one of the authors of the new heresy, but because by his imprudent economy he fostered and encouraged their iniquitous assertions. A distinction is here pointedly drawn between the heretics and Honorius, and the cause of the condemnation of each of the parties is clearly and distinctly stated. We do not understand how these words could be so

⁶⁵ Vita Archiep. P. De Marca scripta a Balutio. In Op. de Marca, ed. Parisiis, 1663, p. 29.
⁶⁶ Papst Fabeln, pp. 138, 139.
⁶⁷ The Condemnation of Pope Honorius, p. 6.
⁶⁸ Liber Diurnus RR. PP. cap. ii. tit. ix. Professio secunda Fidei, p. 52, ed. Migne, t. cv. PP. LL.

far misconstrued as to make them represent Honorius to have been condemned in the same way as Sergius and his followers. What surprises us is that Mr. Renouf quotes the above extract without the least remark, as if it were obvious that it told against Honorius; and he assumes that his readers will extract from it a sense which it evidently excludes.

We must not omit to notice in this place what Mr. Renouf says of the similarity between the texts, both Greek and Latin, of Leo's letter to the Emperor, which we examined above, and another passage of the second profession of faith in the *Liber Diurnus*.[69] We will give the whole of the latter passage: "Eos qui novo et hæretico dogmate immaculatam Dei Ecclesiam polluere nitebantur, et errasse manifestius probaverunt [Patres vi. Synodi], et cum sui erroris auctoribus atque fautoribus perpetuo anathemate damnaverunt."[70] Mr. Renouf produces only one-half of this passage, going no farther than the word "probaverunt;" moreover, he omits the conjunctive particle "et," and prints in italics the word "errasse." All this goes to show that the readers of the pamphlet are intended to conclude that in the second pontifical profession of faith Pope Honorius is judged to have erred, since he is comprehended among those who *immaculatam conabantur corrumpere Ecclesiam*, according to the Latin text of Leo's letter to Constantine. But if

---

[69] The Condemnation of Pope Honorius, p. 13, in note.
[70] Liber Diurnus, l. c. p. 51.

we consider the passage in its entirety, no difficulty will remain on the point. For in the foregoing extract three classes of men are mentioned as condemned by the Sixth Synod: (1.) those who simply *nitebantur corrumpere Ecclesiam novo et hæretico dogmate;* (2.) those who had been *erroris auctores;* (3.) and those who had been in any manner favourable to it, *fautores.* Now, after a few lines, the names are found of those who are designated as condemned by the Council. Here likewise they are distributed into three classes: (1.) *auctores novi hæretici dogmatis,* i. e. Sergius, Pyrrhus, Paul, Peter, Theodore of Pharan, and Cyrus of Alexandria; (2.) *qui pravis eorum assertionibus fomentum impendit,* namely, Honorius alone; (3.) *qui hæretica dogmata contra veritatem fidei synodaliter declaratam atque prædicatam pertinaciter defendebant, cum omnibus hæreticis scriptis atque sequacibus, qui unam execrabiliter asserebant voluntatem et unam operationem in Christo;* and under this head follow the names of Macarius, Stephen, and Polychronius, and others. Now if we contrast the two passages, it will appear evident that Honorius, *qui fomentum impendit,* is not included either in the first or in the second category of the first extract, but only in the third, *fautoribus.* Neither are we forced by the word "fautoribus" to admit in Honorius any intellectual adhesion to error; for the silence of the Pastors of the Church when they ought to raise up their voice against error and heresy, according to the ecclesiastical canons, is to be accounted as an encouragement given to error and heresy. So that the passage in question, far from telling against the purity of Honorius' faith, affords a new confirmation of our assertion.

But let us now examine a passage concerning Honorius' condemnation, which we find in the old Roman Breviary in the lesson for the feast of St. Leo II., the 28th of June.[71]

Mr. Renouf remarks in his pamphlet that "till the seventeenth century the Roman Breviary spoke of the confirmation by Pope Leo II. of the holy Sixth Synod, in which were condemned Cyrus, Sergius, Honorius, Pyrrhus, Paul, and Peter, qui unam voluntatem et operationem in Domino Jesu Christo dixerunt et prædicarunt."[72] We must warn our readers not to fall into a very possible mistake here: it would be incorrect to suppose that the name of Honorius is mentioned in *all* the old Latin Breviaries among the persons condemned by the Sixth Synod. In some very old Breviaries of this country no name at all is found, either of Honorius or of the others condemned in that Council. In the Sarum Breviary of the fourteenth century we read, in the lessons for the feast of St. Leo: "Hic Leo suscepit Sextam Synodum, quæ per Dei providentiam celebrata est, simulque cum eo legati Sedis Apostolicæ et duo Patriarchæ, id est Constantinopolis et Antiochiæ, etiam 150 Episcopi; in qua condemnati sunt hæretici qui

---

[71] In festo S. Leonis Papæ, die 28 Junii, Lect. iv. secundi nocturni.

[72] The Condemnation of Pope Honorius, p. 6.

unam tantum voluntatem et operationem in Domino Jesu Christo dicebant."[73] In the Aberdeen Breviary, which is of the fifteenth century, we find the following words: "Leo suscepit Sextam Synodum intra regium palatium Constantini Magni tum viventis, in qua condemnati sunt hæretici qui dixerunt unam tantum esse voluntatem et operationem in Christo."[74]

As to the Roman Breviary, we think it well to transcribe here the whole passage as it exists in the old Breviary,[75] for Mr. Renouf does not give us the entire extract. It runs as follows: "In qua [Synodo] condemnati sunt Cyrus, Sergius, Honorius, Pyrrhus, Paulus, et Petrus, nec non et Macarius, cum suo discipulo Stephano, sed et Polychronius, Novus, et Simon, qui unam voluntatem et operationem in D. N. J. C. dixerunt vel prædicarunt, aut qui denuo prædicaturi fuerint [fuerant] aut dispensaverint [dispensaverant]."

Now the foregoing words, and the rest of the lessons, are copied word for word from the life of Leo, written by Anastasius,[76] the librarian of the Roman Church, from which also the lessons of the Sarum and Aberdeen Breviaries are taken, with some abridgment, except that in the Roman compilation the words "Novus et Simon" are found by mistake,

---

[73] We quote from a ms. copy of the Sarum Breviary preserved in the library of Stonyhurst College.

[74] Aberdense Breviarium, pars æstiva, fol. x.

[75] We use the two editions of Rome 1478 and Paris 1511.

[76] Historia de Vitis Rom. Pontif. n. lxxxii. ed. Migne, t. cxxviii. PP. LL. p. 847.

instead of "novus Simon," and the word "dispensaverint" for "defensaverint." In the appendix to the lives of the Roman Pontiffs of Anastasius, evidently extracted from the work of the Pontifical librarian, and written in the ninth century, we read in the life of St. Leo the same passage, but without the words "qui unam voluntatem et operationem in D. N. J. C. dixerunt et prædicarunt."[77] Now the question arises, whether Anastasius intended to say that Honorius asserted and defended one will and operation in Christ. In the life of Pope Agatho he relates that, after the sentence of condemnation pronounced by the Sixth Council, "abstulerunt de diptycis Ecclesiarum nomina Patriarcharum, vel de picturis Ecclesiæ figuras eorum, aut in foribus ubi esse poterant, auferentes, id est Cyri, Sergii, Pauli, Pyrrhi, Petri, per quos error orthodoxæ fidei usque nunc pullulavit."[78] Anastasius here suppressed the name of Honorius, evidently because the character of having been the source of the heresy could not be applied to him, but only to the Monothelite Patriarchs. In the appendix mentioned above the anonymous author has transcribed the entire passage without any alteration whatever.[79]

But apart from this, whoever is acquainted with the Collectanea addressed by Anastasius to John the Deacon, and published by the learned Sirmondi, must be aware that the Roman Librarian never

[77] Appendix ad Vitas Romanorum Pontificum, n. lxxxii. ex codice Cap. Veron. (In op. cit. Anastasii, ed. cit. p. 1422.)
[78] Op. cit. Anastasii Bibl. n. lxxxi. p. 811, t. ii. op. ed. Migne.
[79] App. cit. n. lxxxi p. 1422. In t. ii. op. Anastasii, ed. Migne.

harboured the idea that Pope Honorius had said, or taught, or held in any manner, that in Jesus Christ there was only one will and one operation. He calls those "calumniators" who said that Pope Honorius had ever asserted one only will in Christ; and he distinctly maintained that the Pope can by no means be considered as condemned for heresy in the Sixth Synod.[80] Now, after those declarations, how can we believe that Anastasius would simply assert in the life of Leo, without any remark or any mitigating expression, that Pope Honorius had been condemned because of his having denied the two wills and operations in Christ? It might be said that Anastasius in this place represents Honorius as guilty *in solidum* of the same crime with the others, although not in the same manner. But we believe that another explanation of the passage in question may fairly be given. We can venture to say, in the first place, that all the matter relating to the Sixth Synod and the sentences of condemnation it passed is summarised by the author from the letter of Leo to the Emperor Constantine, from which also is taken the portion we have quoted of the second profession of faith in the *Liber Diurnus*. Now Pope Leo in his letter, after anathematising the authors of Monothelism and Pope Honorius himself, for the reason we mentioned above, anathematises Macarius, his disciple Stephen, and Polychronius, whom he calls

[80] "Pro Papa Honorio a calumniatoribus impetito, quod unam D. N. J. C. tantum scripserit voluntatem." Collectanea ad Joannem Diaconum, ed. Migne, t. cxxix. PP. LL. p. 558 seq.

the new Simon, and finally all those who hold the same maxims, and who had dared, or ever should dare, to assert in Christ one will and one operation.[81] Likewise in the second profession of faith in the *Liber Diurnus*, those heretics are first anathematised who had originated the error of Monothelism, and Honorius, who had fostered it by his imprudent economy. Next to these, Macarius, his disciple Stephen, and Polychronius (the new Simon), and finally all their followers, " qui unam execrabiliter asserebant voluntatem et unam operationem in Christo."[82] Now Anastasius in his life of St. Leo carefully distinguished all the categories of persons who had been condemned in the Sixth Council. He merely suppressed the grounds of condemnation stated by St. Leo in his letter to Constantine and in the second profession of faith. But since the last category mentioned in both those documents did not imply any particular person, but, in a general way, all those who either had asserted, or should in future assert, one will and one operation in Christ, therefore Anastasius expressed it by the same words. Again, in the passage in question, the Roman librarian sets before us all the classes of persons who had been condemned by the Sixth Synod, in the same order as that in which they occur in the two

[81] "Ετι δι και τους τα ομοια αυτων φρονησαντας, η φρονουντας τους δηλονοτι εν θελημα και μιαν ενεργειαν φασκειν κατατολμησαντας, &c. Epistola Leonis II. Papæ ad Constantinum Imp. (Labbe, t. vii. p. 1156.)
[82] Liber Diurnus, c. ii. Secunda professio Fidei. (Migne, t. cv. PP. LL. p. 52, 53.)

above-mentioned documents. In the first class he places those who had died before the date of the Council, and among them he mentions Honorius, but without stating the cause of condemnation of any of the number. To the first he subjoins the other class of those who had obstinately defended their error before the Sixth Synod itself (nec non, &c.); in the last place comes the class of those unnamed persons who either had denied, or should ever deny in the future, the two wills and operations in Christ. If Anastasius had put a conjunctive particle between this additional class and the others, as is done by St. Leo in his letter to the Emperor, and by the author of the second profession of faith, the meaning of his words would have been perfectly clear and evident.[63] Mr. Renouf, by quoting only the latter portion of the passage which he found in the Roman Breviary, deprives his readers of the means of discovering the true meaning.

Again, Mr. Renouf complains that "the name

[63] We may quote another passage from the acts of the Council, as an additional confirmation of the foregoing just given. The passage is extracted from the acclamations at the end of the Synod. "Theodoro Pharanitæ anathema; Sergio et Honorio anathema; Pyrrho et Paulo anathema; Cyro et Petro anathema; Macario et Stephano et Polycronio anathema; omnibus hæreticis anathema; qui prædicaverunt et prædicant et docent et docturi sunt unam voluntatem et unam operationem in dispensatione D. N. J. C. anathema." Act. xviii. (Labbe, t. vii. p. 1079). Here again we see the same order kept with regard to the names of those who are anathematised; and the last words, which are very similar to those in question, do not refer to the foregoing names, but imply in a general way all those who either had taught, or were teaching, or would ever teach Monothelism.

of Honorius is no longer to be found in the Breviary, but the other names are still retained;" and he remarks that "it is most unjust to suppress the name of Honorius, and yet retain the other names."[84] The *Union Review*, eulogising the *masterly pamphlet* which we are considering, says that fact alone speaks volumes.[85] Now the remark is founded entirely on error. It is not true that in the Roman Breviary, as reformed by order of the Council of Trent, all the other names were retained. Out of nine, only three were retained; namely Cyrus, Sergius, and Pyrrhus, the very authors and first propagators of Monothelism.[86] The names of Paul, Peter, Macarius, Stephen, and Polychronius, as well as that of Honorius, were expunged, because it was not necessary to state in a short lesson the names of all the heretics condemned in the Council, much less of Honorius, who had not been anathematised for any error whatever, and whom an ignorant reader might have believed to have been condemned for heresy, because his name was found in the same list with some who were undoubtedly condemned for that crime. But what Mr. Renouf adds after the above-quoted words, in order to justify his assertion, is per-

[84] The Condemnation of Pope Honorius, p. 6 and note; Union Review, July 1868, p. 881.

[85] An argument had been founded on this fact more than a hundred and fifty years ago by the Author of the *Defensio Declarationis Cleri Gallicani*, p. ii. l. xii. c. xxvi. t. ii. p. 101. Basileæ, 1730.

[86] See the Lesson iv. of the feast of St. Leo II. on the 28th of June. (Romanum Breviarium, ex Decr. Conc. Trid.)

haps the most absurdly false statement of the many that occur in his ill-starred pamphlet.

"Sergius," he says, "presented his confession to the Pope, who simply approved it; and he died without the slightest intimation from Rome that his doctrine was anything but orthodox. Had he been a perfect Ultramontane, he could not have acted otherwise." So then Mr. Renouf puts Pope Honorius on the same level with Sergius, and represents this latter as orthodox till the time of his death, — the Patriarch, that is, who forged the *libellus* of Mennas to Pope Vigilius, and that of Vigilius to the Emperor Justinian, in order to support his Monothelism; both which documents were condemned by the Sixth Synod as heretical forgeries.[87] But after what we have said in our first three sections, the remark of Mr. Renouf is not worth a further answer.

It now only remains for us to examine the purport of the anathemas inflicted on Honorius by the Councils which followed the Sixth Synod; for the enemies of Pope Honorius, and Mr. Renouf among them, remind us that the Seventh and Eighth Œcumenical Councils joined in the condemnation of Honorius; therefore our writer concludes: "the condemnation for heresy of a Pope by three Œcumenical Councils, and a long series of Roman Pontiffs, is utterly subversive of the theory of Papal Infallibility."[88] We have already destroyed this consequence, by showing,

[87] Concilium vi. act. xiv. (Labbe, t. vii. p. 1014 seq.)
[88] The Condemnation of Pope Honorius, p. 7.

K

not only that no heretical tenet is contained in the letters of Pope Honorius, but also that the Sixth Synod did not condemn him either for any erroneous *ex cathedrâ* teaching, or for any heresy whatever. With regard to the Seventh and Eighth Councils, we again remark, in answer to Mr. Renouf, that even if those Synods had condemned Honorius for heresy, it would not follow from this that the doctrine of Papal Infallibility is untenable, unless it is first shown that Honorius was anathematised for having taught heresy *ex cathedrâ*. Mr. Renouf is quite unable to prove this point, especially when we consider that both these Synods solemnly acknowledged the doctrine of Papal Infallibility; when the Seventh submitted itself unreservedly to the letter of Pope Adrian I., in which that maxim was enforced, and perfect adhesion to it was imposed;[89] and when, in the Eighth, the profession of faith of Pope Adrian II. was unanimously received, in which the previous formulary of Honorius was inserted, declaring that the Catholic doctrine had always been preserved in its integrity in the Roman Apostolic See.[90] We abstain from commenting on these facts, which we shall fully explain in our work upon Papal Infallibility. For the present we limit ourselves to examining whether it is true that the two Councils mentioned really condemned Honorius for heresy. Certainly

[89] Adriani I. Epistola ad Tarasium. In act. ii. Conc. vii., Nicæni ii. (Labbe, t. viii. p. 771 seq.)

[90] Libellus fidei Adriani II. ad Synodum viii. In act. i. Conc. Const. iv. (Œcum. viii. (Labbe, t. x. p. 497.)

Condemnation of Pope Honorius. 131

the Seventh Council has nothing which countenances the assertion. We do not here take notice of several passages of the Seventh Synod in which Honorius' condemnation is mentioned,—as, for instance, in the letter of Tarasius,[91] in that of Theodore,[92] in the *tomus* of the Deacon Epiphanius,[93] and in a letter of Tarasius to the Clergy of Constantinople.[94] These passages are not the utterances of the Synod, and cannot therefore be relied upon to represent its opinion in the matter. The view of the Council may be said to be expressed only in the profession of faith, and in the synodical letter addressed to the Emperor; and in neither of these documents can anything be found against our assertion. In the profession of faith the Fathers of the second Nicene Council declare that they received all the definitions of the Œcumenical Councils; therefore, mentioning the Sixth Synod, they say: "Likewise we profess in Christ two wills and two operations, according to the propriety of His two natures, as the Sixth Synod of Constantinople proclaimed; and we cut off Sergius, Honorius, Cyrus, Pyrrhus, and Macarius, who were not willing to keep faithful to God, and those who follow their mind."[85] Now

[91] Epistola Tarasii Patr. Constant. In act. iii. Conc. Nic. ii. (Labbe, t. viii. p. 813.)
[92] Epist. Theodori Patr. Antioch. In act. iii. cit. (Labbe, l. c. p. 832.)
[93] Tomus secundus Epiphanii Diaconi. In act. vi. Conc. Nic. ii. (Labbe, l. c. p. 1072.)
[94] Epist. Tarasii P.C. ad Clerum Constantinop. In act. vii. Conc. Nic. ii. (Labbe, l. c. p. 1237.)
[85] Terminus Synodi Nicaenae Secundae. In act. vii. (Labbe,

in this passage there is nothing which goes to prove the assertion of Mr. Renouf, that Pope Honorius was anathematised by the Seventh Council as a Monothelite.⁹⁶ The Fathers of Nicæa mention what the Sixth Council did, without characterising the condemnation of those who had been anathematised by the Synod. In the synodical letter they anathematise again all those who had been condemned by the six preceding Councils, and among them Honorius; but they do not specify the crime for which he had been stricken with anathema by the Sixth Synod.⁹⁷ Undoubtedly the words of the Eighth Council are apparently stronger, but do not really carry any greater weight than, the decree of condemnation of the Sixth Synod. In fact, in the Greek compilation of the Acts of the Eighth Council it is said that, "after the canons (sanctioned by the Fathers), the definition was read of the same Eighth and Œcumenical Synod, which comprehends the symbol of faith, the profession of the seven preceding Synods, and the anathemas against those whom the Synods had condemned."⁹⁸ The Eighth Council, therefore, did not intend to pronounce a

---

t. viii. p. 1205.) καθ᾿ ὃν τρόπον καὶ ἡ ἐν Κωνσταντινουπόλει ἕκτη σύνοδος ἐξεβόησιν, ἀποπνύξασα Σέργιον, Ὀνώριον, κ. τ. λ. τοὺς ἀθελήτους τῆς εὐσεβείας καὶ τοὺς τούτων ὁμόφρονας.

⁹⁶ The Condemnation of Pope Honorius, p. 6.

⁹⁷ Concilium Nicænum ii. act. vii. (Labbe, t. viii. p. 1232.) ἀναθεματίσαντες ... Σεργίου, καὶ Ὀνωρίου, καὶ Κύρου, καὶ Πύρρου, καὶ τὴν σὺν αὐτοῖς μονοθέλητον, μᾶλλον δὲ κακοθέλητον βούλησιν.

⁹⁸ Conc. Constantinop. iv. act. x. (Labbe, t. x. ex Actis Græcis, p. 861.)

new sentence against Honorius and the others; nor could the assembled Fathers do it, inasmuch as no conciliar examination had preceded. The words referring to Honorius and the others in the definition cannot, then, have any other meaning than that intended by the Sixth Synod itself,[99] since the Fathers do no more than relate as a matter of history the condemnation of Honorius with the other Eastern Prelates. Now, when speaking of the decree of condemnation pronounced against Honorius in the Sixth Synod, we remarked that, according to the principles of both civil and ecclesiastical law, Honorius can be said to have been guilty *in solidum* of the crime of the others; not because he was a Monothelite, as Sergius and Cyrus, but because by his imprudent policy and grievous negligence he consented to the pollution of the Immaculate Church; because he did not at the first outbreak extinguish the flame of the heretical error, but fostered it by his culpable remissness. No wonder then, if, in the following Councils, he is anathematised, together with the others, *in solidum*. The Fathers of the Seventh and

[99] The words of the Council are as follows, according to the translation of Anastasius: "Anathematizmus Theodorum qui fuit Episcopus Pharan, et Sergium, et Pyrrhum, et Paulum, ac Petrum, impios Præsules Constantinopolitanorum Ecclesiæ, atque cum iis Honorium Romæ, una cum Cyro Alexandriæ, necnon et Macarium Antiochiæ, ac discipulum ejus Stephanum, qui malæ opinionis Apollinarii et Eutychetis et Severi impiorum hæresiarcharum dogmata sectantes, sine operatione ac sine voluntate animatam animâ rationabili et intellectuabili Dei carnem, sensibus læsis, et revera sine ratione prædicaverunt." Conc. Const. iv. act. x. Terminus Sanctæ Synodi. (Labbe, L c. ex Anastasii versione, p. 653.)

of the Eighth Councils might well suppose the history and the details of the condemnations pronounced in the Sixth Synod to be sufficiently known. They had in hand the settlement of perfectly different questions. In their definition, they gave, as was usual, no more than a summary sketch of the tenets and of the condemnations decreed in the preceding Councils, from the acts of which any further explanation and particulars might be gathered. In the passage mentioned above, the Fathers of the Eighth Synod describe in a general way the crime for which the Third of Constantinople pronounced its decree of condemnation in its thirteenth session. But they by no means intended that their words should be applied to Honorius in the same sense as they are applied to Sergius and the others. Otherwise it would have been the solemn proclamation of a calumny to assert that Honorius had maintained that Christ's humanity had no operation, when, in truth, he had pointedly maintained the exact contrary. No; Honorius did not teach that heresy; but by his culpable negligence and imprudent economy of silence he permitted it to be taught and widely spread. He became, therefore, responsible for it, and partook in the crime of its authors. In this sense, and in this sense only, can we receive the words of the Eighth Council, which, if taken in a contrary meaning, would be mendacious and calumnious. Nor can the expressions used by Pope Adrian II., in his third address to the Council, afford the least support to Mr. Renouf's view, since

Adrian II. never asserted that Pope Honorius had been condemned for heresy, but that he had been *super hæresi accusatus*.

The Roman librarian Anastasius, who, as Mr. Renouf tells us, "took an active part in the Eighth Council," does not assert that the Sixth Synod condemned Honorius for heresy, but only that it anathematised him, as if he were a heretic (*quasi hæretico*);[100] that is to say, the Council put him on a par with the others in the severity of its sentence, but not in the crime for which he was condemned. What, then, is the meaning of a Council pronouncing an anathema against a Prelate after his death? It implies nothing but that his name was to be erased from the diptychs, and his likeness from the pictures in the churches; because it was customary, especially from the beginning of the seventh century, for the names of all orthodox Bishops to be inserted in the diptychs, and their portraits exposed in the churches. Now Anastasius relates that, after the sentence of the Sixth Synod, the names of Sergius, Cyrus, Paul, Pyrrhus, and Peter were expunged from the diptychs, and the pictures of them destroyed; but he does not say anything of the name of Honorius having been erased, or of his images being removed from the churches or effaced.[101] His name undeniably is found in the Oriental diptychs,[102] and we still have the lau-

[100] Collectanea Epist. ad Joannem, l. c. t. iii. op. p. 559, ed. Migne.
[101] Vitæ RR. PP. Vita Agathonis Papæ, ed. Migne, op. t. ii. p. 811.
[102] "Honorium Pontificem in Orientalium diptychis inscriptum

The Sixth Synod.

datory notices which accompanied his name.[103] All things tend to corroborate the view that the severe sentence pronounced by the Sixth Synod against that Pope was tempered in its execution, because he had not been condemned for heresy.

---

vidimus," says Baronius in Annalibus, an. 681, n. liv. t. viii. p. 622, ed. Coloniæ.

[103] See them in Baronius, op. cit. an. 636. n. ii. seq. t. viii. p. 638 seq.

CONCLUSION.

The chief argument of those who have at any time disputed Papal Infallibility, is the fall and condemnation of Pope Honorius. Many Gallican writers made this the key of their whole position, differing in this from the Jansenists, who sought to secure an argument against the infallibility of the Church on dogmatic facts by vindicating the orthodoxy of Honorius. Dr. Döllinger and Mr. Renouf have in their pamphlets again dressed up the old story of the fall of Honorius and his condemnation as a means of attack against Papal Infallibility, and an instrument for restoring, if possible, that illogical system of Gallicanism which should be condemned by every learned and impartial man. The *Union Review* of July last (1868) agrees, and extols to the skies the *masterly pamphlet* of Mr. Renouf, of which it expresses its doubts whether Honorius' lapse and condemnation "has ever been exhibited so clearly and fully or with such crushing force as here."[1] Certainly Mr. Renouf has shown great cleverness in having summed up in twenty-six pages, without a single omission, all the mistakes and errors usually made by those who have written against Honorius, and added, moreover, no small number of his own. At all events, we have proved to demonstration what

[1] Union Review, July 1868, p. 381.

Catholic theologians hold for certain—that Honorius' letters did not contain anything which can fairly be construed as an utterance *ex cathedrâ*; and that the Sixth Council did not condemn him for anything like an *ex cathedrâ* teaching of error. This would have been sufficient to blunt the edge of a weapon which our adversaries have continually used against Papal Infallibility. But it would not have been sufficient to do justice to Pope Honorius, nor to satisfy the claims of gratitude towards him. In this country the memory of Pope Honorius should be held in immortal honour, and his name arouse feelings of veneration and gratitude. He was the happy heir of the glorious work begun by the great Gregory on behalf of this nation. He encouraged with his paternal letters Edwin, the powerful King of Northumbria, to hold out in defence of Christianity against the swelling tide of paganism, and to bear in mind the affection and instructions given by his illustrious predecessor.[2] He it was that confirmed with his apostolic words Paulinus, who had been sent by St. Gregory to preach to the Northumbrians; and he it was that rewarded the Saint for his glorious success with the pallium.[3] It was this great Pope that consoled and supported the missionaries occupied with the conversion of the Angles and East Saxons, and in an especial manner his namesake Honorius, archbishop of Canterbury, who was at the head of that evangelical enterprise, and who also

---

[2] Beda, Historia Ecclesiastica, L. ii. c. xvii. ed. Migne, op. t. vi. pp. 109, 110.   [3] Ib. L. c. p. 109.

deserved to receive the pallium at the hands of the same Pontiff.⁴ Moreover, whilst he laboured to give new vigour to Christianity in those parts of England where it had been already introduced by the zeal of St. Gregory, he did not forget the portion of the Saxon nation which was still lying in the darkness of paganism. He sent a new apostle, Birinus, to preach the gospel to the warlike people of Wessex, and to withstand the idolatry of Mercia, which threatened to overflow and sweep away Christianity from the north and the east of the island.⁵ Bede, the most learned man who appeared among the Saxons in the seventh and eighth century, knew well how to appreciate the virtues of Pope Honorius. In his Ecclesiastical History of the English nation he represented Honorius as a perfect pastor ;⁶ but in the life of the Abbot Bertolf he speaks at length in his praise. He calls him a holy and venerable Pontiff, clear-sighted and resolute, illustrious for his learning, and of remarkable meekness and humility.⁷ And although in his work *De Ratione Temporum* he mentions his condemnation by the Sixth Synod, he abstains from adding any remark whatever tending to cast a slur on the memory of the Pontiff.⁸ If

⁴ Beda, l. c. et c. xviii. p. 111 seq.
⁵ Ib. l. iii. c. vii. p. 126 seq.
⁶ See the places quoted above from Bede's history.
⁷ Beda, Vita S. Bertolfi Abbatis, op. t. iii. ed. Basileæ, p. 344. "Sanctus Papa . . . . . erat venerabilis præsul Honorius, sagax animo, vigens consilio, doctrina clarus, dulcedine et humilitate pollens," &c.
⁸ Beda, De Ratione Temporum, c. lxvi. p. 567, 568, op. t. i. ed. Migne.

Mr. Renouf, in the *extensive studies* he has made of ecclesiastical literature, had met with these facts and reflected upon them, he would not have forgotten the regard due to a Pope, to whose paternal and apostolic endeavours, after Gregory the Great, England is indebted for its conversion to Christianity. Even if Pope Honorius had been condemned for heresy, gratitude for benefits received from him should have suggested moderation and forbearance to an Englishman when forced to speak on the subject. But when justice and gratitude are on the same side, the tone which it is fitting to take is less easily mistaken.

Having taken in hand the full discussion of the cause of Pope Honorius, and the vindication of him from all heresy whatever, it was our duty to examine the doctrine contained in his letters, and to inquire into the opinion which his contemporaries had formed of his orthodoxy. But beyond this, we have made a principal subject of our inquiry the condemnation pronounced by the Sixth Council, in order to show its purport, and the nature of the fault for which Honorius was condemned. We have willingly gone into this inquiry at some length, not only because the justification of Honorius principally depends upon it, but also because by clearing him from every imputation of heresy we strike at the very root of the argument of the adversaries of Papal Infallibility, and wrest from them that scrap of ground on which they strive to make good their footing. The general persuasion of men of the greatest ability and learning, both of the present and of the preceding century, is in our favour, and the few exceptions are of no value in the matter; especially if we take into account their want of solid learning, their prejudices, and the passionate and bitter temper in which they write. Dr. Döllinger, who tried to call in question the almost unanimous opinion of Catholic writers in favour of Pope Honorius' orthodoxy, was answered by F. Schneeman, who not only clearly proved his own assertion, but also exposed the distortions and misrepresentations by which the Munich professor had endeavoured to draw under his own flag theologians who stood in the opposite ranks.[9] In our own argument we have not had recourse to the expedient of raising suspicions of forgery; we throw no doubt on the genuineness of any of the existing documents which bear upon the question. We have admitted them, and as they exist in their original language, although we cannot feel sure that the Greek translation of the original letters of Honorius represents accurately the literal meaning of each expression they contained. We have acknowledged that Honorius was in fault, and we have pointed out precisely what his fault was, in accordance with the very documents which our adversaries produce. In this manner we have maintained the justice of the decree pronounced by the Sixth Synod against Honorius, while at the same time we do not approve a certain want of considera-

[9] See his pamphlet, Studien über die Honorius-Frage, von G. Schneeman S. J.; Freiburg, 1864.

tion for the memory of the deceased Pontiff, and some bitterness of feeling manifested by the Oriental Prelates. But though thus admitting his fault, we have been far from making any charge of secret corruption of intention against the Pontiff. Nor was this necessary in order to justify the sentence of the Œcumenical Council; for the axiom, *Ecclesia non judicat de internis*, is to be applied to all the judgments of the coercive power of the Church. Nor are we even forced to believe that Honorius either remained till death unaware of his fault, or that, if he became aware of it, he did not expiate it by true satisfactory penance. Long before the Sixth Synod assembled, the Fifth Council had decided in the affirmative the question, whether it were lawful to anathematise, even for heresy, persons who had died in the communion of the Church. Accordingly, it anathematised Theodore, Theodoret, and Ibas, with their writings, although they had submitted to the Confession of Faith sanctioned at Chalcedon, and had been declared orthodox by the Council. The Church, as we remarked above, when condemning persons who have already gone before the judgment-seat of God, cannot mean to influence the sentence already pronounced on them by the Eternal Judge. Nor does the sentence of the Church give any certainty of their having been condemned by Christ. The Church condemns the fault they committed in their lifetime, as it appeared before her tribunal; she strikes their names from the diptychs, and erases their figures from the churches, in order to repair the evil consequences of their faults, and to caution their successors against falling into the same crimes.

Such is the method and such are the principles on which we have written this essay. As to Mr. Renouf, we cannot say what his leading principles are; but we are sure that no true English Catholic will congratulate him on his scandalous pamphlet against the memory of Pope Honorius. Mr. Renouf, as it appears from his writing, wants to produce division amongst the Catholics of this country by bringing into popular use the Gallican distinction between Ultramontanes and non-Ultramontanes. But true and sincere Catholics reject and condemn a distinction, the invention of a degenerate party in the truly Catholic French nation, and serving only to adulterate the true idea of Catholicism. And "Catholic" is the only name which is or ever can be properly applied to the children of the one true Church, to distinguish them from all sects whatever. All who are not with them in the unity of one Faith and one Pastor are against them, and cannot be entitled to that denomination. But those only are in their communion, in the communion of the Catholic Church, who follow in all things the Apostolic See, and profess all its doctrines, and entirely submit to all its decisions:[10] the others are false brethren, who may have crept into the Church in order to spread scandal and to encourage discord;

---

[10] See the dogmatic formula of faith imposed by Hormisdas on the Orientals after the Acacian schism.

but not in order to spread the Gospel, and to extend the mystical Body of Christ. The word *Ultramontane*, applied to those Catholics who believe in Papal Infallibility, is in our times an insult to the Catholic faith; for the doctrine of Papal Infallibility is not an opinion of a party, who incline to exaggerated notions of Papal prerogatives; it is not an offspring of the Isidorian Decretals; but it is the doctrine of the Apostolic See, the doctrine of Pius IX., as well as of all the Popes who, in the first century, gave witness to the divinity of their faith with their own blood; it is the doctrine of the Episcopate of the Catholic Church; which men full of a spirit of party tried to stamp out in the Church, in order that they might substitute in its place the infallibility of the state and of the civil ruler.[11] We can easily bear that the Voltaire-taught courtiers in France should give the name of Ultramontanes to the Catholic defenders of the privileges of the Holy See; but it is hard to bear that insult from a man who professes to be a Catholic and an obedient child of the Church.

But Mr. Renouf, in a most objectionable Gallican spirit, not only maintains that the Pope is subject to

[11] See the remarks on the first rise of Gallicanism in *The Pope and the Church*, p. i. sect. vii. p. 157 seq. The body of the Catholic Bishops expressly professed the doctrine of Papal Infallibility in the address presented by them with their signatures to Pius IX. on the occasion of the centenary of St. Peter. Moreover, the Bishops of different countries, especially of France, assembled in provincial Synod, have unanimously adopted and professed that doctrine in the course of this century. See Die kirchliche Lehrgewalt, von G. Schneeman, iv. p. 202 seq., p. 138 seq. Freiburg in Brisgau, 1868.

the General Council, and would strip him both of his infallibility and of the power he holds independently of the Catholic Episcopate; it seems that he considers the head of the Church to be bound to obey the civil authority in the administration of the Church. For what else does he mean when he says that, "among other ignorant assertions which have been common of late, it has been said that Popes have never acknowledged themselves subject to human sovereigns, and that Christian sovereigns have never claimed authority over Popes"?[12] Does he mean that some writers have asserted that the Popes nowhere acknowledge themselves subject to Christian Emperors in temporal matters? If so, we answer that such an opinion would not deserve any notice, far less so long a notice in a short pamphlet on a totally different argument. We are not aware that any writer has ever upheld the civil independence of the Pope. But if any has done so, he certainly shows great want of knowledge of civil and ecclesiastical history. And further, if Mr. Renouf meant no more than this, why did he mention the circumstance of Charlemagne having been *adored* by Pope Leo, according to the Eastern practice, in proof of submission of the Pontiff to the Emperor? When Leo III. met Charlemagne, the Popes had already possessed their temporal dominion as independent sovereigns for at least forty-five years.[13] Neither did the coronation

---

[12] The Condemnation of Pope Honorius, p. 1 note.

[13] We count here from the year 754, when the territory, which the Lombards overran, was restored by King Pepin to the Pope.

of the founder of the Carlovingian dynasty as head
of the Holy Empire affect in the smallest degree the
temporal power and independence of the Pope. Mr.
Renouf ought to be acquainted with these facts,
which are fundamental in the history of the Middle
Ages. Nevertheless, we have reason to think that
Mr. Renouf means a total dependence of the Popes
upon the Emperors, extending even to ecclesiastical
matters. We are the more inclined to this view of
his meaning, because, as we remarked above, he is so
anxious to make us believe that the Emperor Constantine was the true president of the Sixth Synod,
and interfered authoritatively in its proceedings. If
this is his meaning, he is altogether mistaken, as there
is abundant evidence to show. All the pretentious
quotations of his note prove nothing. The passages
of St. Agatho's letter to the Emperor either regard
the submission of Rome to the civil power of the
Emperor, or are mere set expressions of civility in
use at the time. Modern urbanity has not wholly
discarded the like, and the Popes were in the habit
of using such phrases in their letters to the Emperors: their object was to show their humble devotion
to the civil power in temporal matters, without, however, giving up any portion of their spiritual independence in the administration of the Church. But
it is more strange that Mr. Renouf should quote the
Novels of Justinian, and particularly the 123d, in
proof of his assertion. He fancies he has found an
unanswerable argument when he has said that, in
this law, the Emperor Justinian lays commands upon

the Archbishops and Patriarchs of the old as well as of the new Rome. But what are the injunctions contained in this passage, or in any part of the collection of the imperial laws? Nothing else than that they should have care to secure the due promulgation and observance of the laws of the Empire.[14] In this Novel, indeed, the Emperor Justinian intends to sanction, and therefore to adopt as state laws, all the canons and customs of the Church concerning the privileges of the Clergy, and to enforce their observance as imperial laws. In those days the deadly principle of divorce between Church and State was unheard of; therefore the Emperors, according to the duty of their protectorship of the Church, gave a uniform sanction to all the ecclesiastical laws; so that, the State being closely united to the Church and sharing in her principle of life, all who had offended against the Church by breach of her canons, should at the same time incur penalties at the hands of the civil power. The Patriarchs and the Roman Pontiff also, before the eighth century, were considered as Imperial Vicars, to whom the Imperial laws were entrusted for their promulgation and observance. This is the reason for which, in the other extract which Mr. Renouf quotes from St. Gregory's Epistles, the holy Pontiff says: "Ego

---

[14] Novella cxxiii. Epilogus. In Corpore Juris Civilis, p. iii. p. 566, ed. Lipsiæ 1865. "Tua igitur gloria, quæ hac lege in perpetuum valitura Serenitas nostra sancivit, per omnia observari curet, et ad omnium notitiam edictis in hac regia civitate propositis perducat."

148   *Conclusion.*

quidem jussioni subjectus .... quæ debui exsolvi," *i.e.* with regard to the promulgation of an imperial law issued by Maurice. But again, the Emperor, by his sanction, did not give any intrinsic authority to the canons of the Church. On this account the Imperial Codes inform us that the civil laws are grounded on the ecclesiastical prescriptions, and that they follow and lean on them.[15] The Emperors regarded as divinely enacted what had been decreed by the Apostolic authority.[16] Therefore they received the sacred canons or decrees of the Church as laws of the Empire;[17] and declared all civil laws to be null and void of effect when they contradicted the laws enacted by the Church.[18] The Emperors, when acting according to the maxims of the public law of that age, never attempted to legislate in the Church, but only to be the guardians and protectors of her laws and constitutions.[19] This certainly does not mean that the Christian Emperors ever claimed authority over the Popes in the spiritual and ecclesiastical order; especially as they expressly distinguished the two

---

[15] Novel. lxxxiii. c. i. l. c. p. 382; Novel. cxxxiii. Præf. l. c. p. 601; Novel. cxxxvii. c. ii. l. c. p. 626, &c.

[16] "Constat esse cælitus constitutam quidquid apostolica decernit auctoritas." Rescriptum Justiniani Imp. ad Dacianum Africanum Episc. (penes Baronium, Annales, an. 541, n. xi. p. 380, t. vii. ed. Coloniæ.)

[17] Novel. vi. c. i. § 8, l. c. p. 36; Novel. cxxiii. c. xxii. l. c. p. 354; Novel. cxxxi. c. i. l. c. p. 593, &c.

[18] Codex Just. l. i. tit. ii. lex xii. In Corpore Juris Civilis, p. ii. ed. cit. p. 16.

[19] In Rescripto cit. ad Dacianum, Novel. cxxxvii. Proœmium. l. c. ed. cit. p. 624.

Conclusion.

orders, ecclesiastic and civil, and the different offices annexed to each of them.[20] But we do not intend here to treat this matter, which is not connected with our argument, and which would itself furnish material for an entire volume. Our object is only to cast a passing glance on the subject, in order to caution Mr. Renouf not again to trouble his countrymen with his *ignorant assertions* (they are his own words) on matters to which he ought to give far more study before he ventures to speak so dogmatically. We are sorry that a man whose natural gifts and acquirements might have enabled him to do good service to the Church's cause in England, should have misused his talents in the composition of a pamphlet which cannot possibly have any effect beyond that of filling the Church with scandal and discord.

[20] Novel. vi. præf. l. c. ed. cit. p. 34. "Maxima inter homines sunt dona Dei a supera benignitate data, sacerdotium et imperium, quorum illud quidem divinis inservit, hoc vero humanas res regit, carumque curam gerit."

THE END.